The Archaeology of the New Testament

E.M. BLAIKLOCK

Thomas Nelson Publishers
Nashville • Camden • New York

Published in Nashville, Tennessee, by Thomas Nelson, Inc. and distributed in Canada by Lawson Falle, Ltd., Cambridge, Ontario.

Printed in the United States of America.

Unless otherwise noted, all Scripture quotations are from the NEW KING JAMES VERSION. Copyright © 1979, 1980, 1982, Thomas Nelson, Inc., Publishers.

Library of Congress Cataloging in Publication Data

Blaiklock, E. M.
    The archaeology of the New Testament.

    Includes index.
    1. Bible. N.T.—Antiquities. I. Title.
BS2375.B49   1984   225.9'3   84-20682
ISBN 0-8407-5889-8

CONTENTS

INTRODUCTION

Archaeology is variously defined. Satisfactory definition often requires description. This is notably the case with archaeology, which has developed as a science over little more than a century. Archaeology began as exciting treasure hunts, in which man ravaged the ancient lands for spectacular and financially valuable memorials of human culture. Today the objects of investigation are much more comprehensive and widespread. From the care with which the very chalk marks on a street wall of Pompeii are preserved to the minute accuracy with which fragments from a Qumran Cave are measured, marks the widening scope and the advancing method of the archaeologist, making definition in some ways simpler and in others more difficult.

Consider an eighty-year-old definition from the *Century Dictionary*: "Archaeology is that branch of knowledge which takes cognizance of past civilizations, and investigates their history in all fields, by means of the remains of art, architecture, monuments, inscriptions, literature, language, customs, and all other examples which have survived." This definition is quite inadequate today. R. A. S. Macalister's definition is half a century old and is much too circumscribed: "Archaeology is the branch of knowledge which has to do with the discovery and classification of the common objects of life."

Perhaps some such definition as the following might be risked: "Archaeology is that branch of historical research that draws its evidence from surviving material traces and remains of past hu-

1

man presence and activity." Such a statement allows room for the increasing scope of archaeological investigation, if only because modern techniques continually render significant hitherto neglected evidence. From aerial photography to Carbon 14 dating, the archaeologist has multiplied and improved his tools and methods, and these developments show no signs of abating.

The vast increase in historical knowledge thus achieved is one of the wonders of this century. When Samuel Johnson remarked in his pontifical fashion some two centuries ago, saying that "all that is really known of the ancient state of Britain is contained in a few pages, and we can know no more than the old writers have told us," he was representing the attitudes of his day. To be sure, when he talked in the George Inn of Fleet Street, Roman London lay beneath his feet, with part of its surviving wall within five minutes walk of his house, up the narrow lane across the street; but the eighteenth century had not learned to read the record in the soil. We know far more of early Italy than Virgil knew, for all the acuteness of archaeological awareness that he displays in Book 8 of his *Aeneid*. We know incomparably more of prehistoric Greece than did Thucydides, in spite of the insight into the unrecorded past he displays in the first chapters of his remarkable history of the Peloponnesian War.

Before archaeological research began to make contributions to biblical studies, supplementary sources for the history contained in the Old and New Testaments were exceedingly scarce. But now, thanks to the probing spade, there exists a great body of texts and artifacts that greatly enrich our understanding of the Bible and the history and teaching it contains. Indeed, our knowledge of the Bible has been transformed.

The archaeology of the New Testament developed somewhat later than other areas in the field. The following chapters will show some of its beginnings in the work of Grenfell, Hunt, and Ramsay at the close of the last century. Its discoveries do not contain the dramatic moments such as those Layard enjoyed when the sand fell away from the winged bulls of Nineveh, when Woolley found the headdress of the royal lady of Ur, or when Garstang first saw the stones of Jericho.

2

And yet drama does not need stage properties so vast or strange. It was surely a moment of high triumph for Hunt when he deciphered the Greek work KARPHOS (a mote) on a scrap of papyrus, and knew that he held a sheet of the sayings of Christ almost contemporary with the writing of the Gospels; or, indeed, for the Abbé Cumont, when he was first confronted with the stone slab from Nazareth.

Glance back at Macalister's definition of archaeology quoted above. "The discovery and classification of the common objects of life" goes far to cover its activities in the study of New Testament archaeology, which sometimes appears to have no other major task. Its stock in trade is discarded paper, the humble gravestone, the petty inscription. Its future work will have little to do with the ruins of city and palace, and the burial of kings; it will leave to others the more pretentious monuments of the ancient world, and build its future story around such "common objects of life" as the Christian lamp, which was found at Caerleon in 1955, the Christian grave relics of the York Museum, the chapel murals in the Lullingstone villa, or the fragment of the Fourth Gospel, found in 1935, which moved back the manuscript tradition of that famously vindicated book to within a generation of its author. It will find a widening sphere in the closer investigation of the catacombs; it will join hands with the Roman historian in the elucidation of life in the highly Christianized provinces of Asia and North Africa. Papyri, still unearthed or undeciphered, will no doubt have much to offer. The discovery of the famous Dead Sea Scrolls in 1947 shows what possibilities lie here.

The spade has obviously not yet finished with the Bible. "I believe in the spade," said Oliver Wendell Holmes. "It has fed the tribes of mankind. It has furnished them water, coal, iron, and gold. And now it is giving them truth—historic truth, the mines of which have never been opened till our time."

E. M. Blaiklock
Auckland, New Zealand
June 1983

1

A LOOK AT THE EVIDENCE

Biblical archaeology held the attention of the world in the middle decades of the last century. Napoleon's eastern strategy had first made both France and England aware of the romance of Egypt's long and storied past. The Rosetta Stone, which opened the way to Egyptology, was a prize of that conflict. The other great Middle Eastern empires, under whose trampling armies the lands of the Bible lay, came into view as excitingly and on as grand a scale as Egypt. There were the cities of Babylon and Assyria, with ziggurats to match the pyramids, art to rival that of Egypt, great libraries of baked clay tablets, and languages for ingenious decipherment.

The world watched a forgotten age emerging, its relics and remains clumsily exposed, ravenously looted, and torn from time and context. Elgin's Parthenon marbles were rescued from ruin and housed well in the British Museum. The same zeal erected Thutmose's obelisk by London's river to decay in London's smog and to be scarred by a zeppelin bomb. Modern man had found a vanished past and hung its spoils above his portals.

The raw material of New Testament archaeology belongs to a more fragile world. To be sure it has its ruined cities, from Corinth, Ephesus, and the towns of the old province of Asia, to Capernaum, and the villages of Galilee. In its wider sweep it has awesome remains like the fortress of Masada and the catacombs of Rome, but much of its material comes to us as an accident of climate, from Egyptian burial grounds and rubbish heaps uninvaded by moisture and from arid Dead Sea caves.

5

The Rosetta Stone.

Fortunately, by the end of the nineteenth century, well past the age of the great "excavators," when scholars became aware of the wealth of knowledge to be won from mere waste paper, archaeology had matured. It has become a science drawing aid from a score of other disciplines and technologies and, for all the dire preoccupations of a war-ridden age, has expanded along with them. In lands as remote as those of the southwest Pacific archaeology has transformed all understanding of the past. And that is why the theme of this book must begin with the invention of papyrus, the ancestor of paper, that frail vehicle by which so much language, literature, and history has been transmitted from age to age.

A man's immortality, as the Roman polymath and aristocrat,

the Elder Pliny remarked, depends upon the amount of paper he can contrive to fill. And of the Elder Pliny his nephew the Younger Pliny said, he had the distinction of "doing things worth writing about and writing things worth reading." Few attain both, but it was true of the old scientist who, while in charge of the Roman flotilla at Misenum, died of his own curiosity in the eruption of Vesuvius in the late summer of A.D. 79. Amid his many volumes of manifold information, Pliny had much to say about papyrus.

Paper in History

The genius who invented paper is not known. He was probably an Egyptian, who must forever stand in fame with the Phoenician who observed that the sounds of human speech could be reduced to a couple of dozen signs. Both were notable benefactors of humankind. Exactly when the great emancipation came to the communication devices of man with the invention of the papyrus sheet and roll is not recorded. The change in the first book of the Bible, from the compacted style of the first eleven chapters to the more expansive narrative of the later stories, could register a movement from baked clay tablets dating from Abraham's day to papyrus records set down by Joseph's scribes and meticulously preserved by Moses when he put the Pentateuch together.

Most of the mass of surviving papyrus documents comes from Greek and Roman Egypt, that is from Alexander's day three centuries before Christ to the time of the Moslem conquest. The Egyptians themselves, however, had used the papyrus roll long before, without providing a clue about its first invention. For example, the Amarna Tablets, official records of the strange Pharaoh, Akhenaton, whose reign ended in the middle of the fourteenth century B.C., were incised clay after the Babylonian fashion. From two or three centuries later comes a papyrus roll that tells amusingly the story of the temple steward, Wenamon, who went to Byblos to negotiate a purchase of fine cedar for a funeral barge. Part of the trade deal with the wily Phoenician prince, Zakar-Baal, was to consist of five hundred rolls of high-grade papyrus. The Egyptians, apt pupils in bureaucracy at least since Joseph's day, probably had begun to realize the value of their virtual monopoly on the papyrus reed. Wenamon confronted an equally powerful monopoly on Lebanon cedar. Zakar-Baal also displayed ledgers and records of a long period of Egyptian trade. On papyrus? Most likely, though the writing material could have been leather.

The *cyperus papyrus*, a species of sedge, was the gift of the Nile. It grew in profusion in the fens and marshlands of the untamed river. Where drainage and irrigation dried out the land and contracted the river's overflow, the reed retreated. "Can the papyrus grow up

Papyrus plants.

A papyrus letter (front).

without a marsh?" asked Job (8:11), quoting a proverb; and in few other parts of the world was there mud like the mire of Egypt. The papyrus once flourished in Lake Huleh of northern Israel, but it disappeared when that fen became a deep-soiled and fertile plain. The immense rush was to Egypt what the bamboo was to China. The baby Moses was entrusted to a tiny papyrus canoe. Egyptians built ships and houses from it, made sails, clothes, ropes. They chewed papyrus in plugs like gum. It was a motif in art. It was a symbol of the land.

The papyrus sheet was made in two layers, the grain of the fibers laid crosswise in warp and woof. The largest stems were about nine inches in diameter, and when sliced finely gave the widest and naturally the most expensive sheets. The two layers were hammered and rolled together until they cohered, bound by their own sap. Some writers stated that Nile water was necessary to provide an effective adhesive, but this was no doubt a legend invented to protect the industry from competition. The local river water could hardly have done more than discolor the product. Of course, the manufacturers aimed at an ivory white surface. To this end the sheets were dried and polished with pumice until they were clean and receptive, without blotting, of the scribe's reed pen dipped in an ink made of soot and glue. The sheets could be gummed into rolls of up to thirty feet. Beyond that they were inconvenient to handle. Luke's two books and John's Gospel probably needed rolls of up to twenty-five feet.

A papyrus letter (back).

The Industry

In Greek and Roman Egypt, a rigid and omnipresent bureaucracy prescribed the width and nature of the finished product, making the industry the most carefully ordered and regulated activity in the world until late imperial times when bureaucracy went mad. To own a papyrus swamp was wealth. Among the scores of documents on the trade that survive are contracts for lease and sale with conservation and management clauses woven in with a complexity of detail modern commerce could hardly better.

One such document dates from 5 B.C., very near the birth of Christ, and it is a monument of legal throroughness and bureaucratic wordiness. It is in Greek and dates from the days of Greek and Roman control of that key land of Mediterranean imperialism. It specifies in detail owners and lessees.

The lessor, Dionysia, signed on behalf of her son, a minor. Boundaries and previous owners of the marshland were mentioned with the most exact definition. Amounts, dates, and installments, along with responsibility for expenses and the nature of the currency were set down. For example, the deed stated: "It shall not be lawful for them to pay the workmen employed more than the current wages. They shall make an extra annual payment of a thousand loads of papyrus with six bundles in each."

There followed regulations for the systematic working of the property and directions for cutting.

> They shall not use pickaxes nor gather immature rushes, nor cut from boats. They shall not sell articles made from papyrus, nor sublet the area to others', nor pasture their own or others' cattle in the marsh and shall remove any stray cattle at their own expense.

A passage follows with a gap or two in the wording, but which clearly had to do with the maintenance of entrance cuttings and canals, filling disused ditches, and restoring banks. The lessees, and not Dionysia, the owner, were to be liable for all damage or loss caused by war, inundation, or governmental action, or any circumstances natural or supernatural.

Any failure to pay on due dates or to infringe any conditions of the lease was to merit imprisonment, fine, and summary eviction, with complete freedom for Dionysia to appropriate all owing to her in rent, damage, or expense from the lessees' resources.

> But if they fulfill the contract in accordance with the conditions herein laid down, Dionysia shall give them undisturbed possession of the lease for the stated period, and allow them to appropriate the fruits of it, and not evict them within the prescribed period, nor demand further payment. Otherwise she herself shall forfeit the damages and costs and a similar penalty as if under order of the Court.

The document concluded with the formula: "We request endorsement," no doubt an application to the local board of control for the registration of the lease. Hierax and Papus, the lessees, surely signed with a small measure of trepidation. This document shows the high value set upon papyrus and gives a glimpse of the regulation-ridden world that saw the Holy Family trudge wearily to Bethlehem, the ancestral home of both Joseph and Mary.

The Ptolemies, the Greek dynasty that ruled Egypt for almost three centuries after the division of Alexander's short-lived empire, undoubtedly took over a very live and functioning bureaucracy. Joseph's achievement for his royal master is proof enough for that (Gen. 47:13-26). The Romans, who were not doctrinaire in matters of government, took over intact any functioning system. Hence their tolerance of the Herods. Dismantling the existing control of the papyrus industry was unlikely. Pliny reported that the Emperor Claudius himself, quite in accordance with his interest in such details of rule, drew up some new regulations for the papyrus industry.

Claudius, ridiculed for his spastic peculiarities, was, in fact, a clever and learned man, and more aware than most of the part paper played in the affairs of the Empire. Pliny reported:

> The thin paper of the period of Augustus was not strong enough to stand the friction of the pen, and moreover, as it let the writing show through, there was a fear of a smudge being caused by what was written on the back, and the great transparency of the paper had an unattractive look in other respects. Consequently the foundation was

made of leaves of second quality and the woof or cross layer of leaves of the first quality. Claudius also increased the width of the sheet, making it a foot across. There were also eighteen-inch sheets called *macrocola*, but examination detected a defect in them, as tearing off a single strip damaged several pages. On this account Claudius' paper has come to be preferred to all other kinds.

Commonsense motivated this check on the zeal of some manufacturers to produce a light and elegant paper. At the same time Claudius' order was an early example of the suffocating bureaucracy, which archaeology has revealed as a feature of the great Roman system for the next four centuries.

Emperor Claudius (A.D. 41-54).

The Emergence of Papyrology

Preoccupied with more visible memorials of the past, the world did not recognize until the end of the nineteenth century what treasures lay hidden in the sand dunes that covered the remains of such towns as Oxyrhynchus, the modern Behnesa, some ten miles west of the Nile. A practically zero rainfall had left the papyrus relics of the town's activity intact.

Papyrus is fragile and rots in high humidity, but in arid conditions it endures almost indefinitely. Although brittle, it remains readable to those trained in palaeography, the decipherment of ancient written scripts. *Papyrology*, the study of papyrus texts, is a new word, used first in 1898, somewhat apologetically in a review of a British Museum catalogue.

References to papyrus documents go back to the eighteenth century and are scattered through the sparse records of early nineteenth-century archaeology, but amazingly it was not until the last decade of that century that systematic search and preservation began. Some names and discoveries stand out. Sir Flinders Petrie, one of the pioneers of scientific archaeology, was excavating an ancient cemetery at Gurob, Egypt, and found that a number of otherwise uninteresting mummies were wrapped in Greek literary texts from a discarded library, dating from the third century before Christ. This was in the winter of 1889 and 1890. There were pages of Plato from two dialogues, written down within a century of that great Athenian philosopher's death, some Homer, a hundred lines of a lost tragedy of Euripides, and many other literary texts.

About the same time the British Museum acquired a parcel of papyrus rolls from the Egyptologist, Sir Wallis Budge. Sir Frederic Kenyon, later chief librarian of the British Museum, was entrusted with the task of examining and identifying this batch. On January 30, 1890, he began the task. The manuscripts were arranged on long tables under glass. With mounting excitement over the following weeks, wrestling with the strange and difficult handwriting, Kenyon discovered known and unknown pages of Greek literature, notably a lost work of Aristotle on the constitution of Athens.

Such discoveries in the field of Greek classical and post-classical literature sprinkled the following decades. In 1956, the collection of the sayings of Christ, popularly known as the *Gospel of Thomas*, was brought precariously out of Egypt in the midst of the tragic Suez crisis. In 1959, a lost play of Menander, the Greek writer of comedies whom Paul quotes ("evil company corrupts good habits"—1 Cor. 15:33), appeared in Geneva. From Menander, also, the two Romans, Plautus and Terence, drew their plots. The witty Greek chalked up his last triumph when the play *Dyscolos*, or *The Grumpy Man*, appeared in the "Third Programme" of the BBC.

The discoveries continue. The lively School of History, Philosophy, and Politics in Sydney's Macquarie University buys for study parcels of fragmentary papyri. Numerous facts have been discovered and meticulously published. I was there soon after they found themselves in possession of what seems to be the oldest manuscript of a tiny portion of the *Acts of the Apostles* in existence, a two- or three-inch shred from chapter 2. At the same time a new Greek word appeared meaning "rushcutters." The fragment must have come from such a document as Dionysia's lease, which was cited earlier.

The Papyri and the New Testament

James Hope Moulton produced the *Prolegomena* to his *Grammar of New Testament Greek* in 1906 and began work on the second volume almost immediately. Not until 1975 was the final volume produced by Nigel Turner. Moulton's fine introductory volume itself demonstrated what the discovery of the nonliterary papyri had done for New Testament studies. He quoted the notable New Testament scholar J.B. Lightfoot, who as early as 1863 had remarked: "...if we could only recover letters that ordinary people wrote to each other without any thought of being literary, we should have the greatest possible help for the understanding of the New Testament generally." The hope was fulfilled within a generation.

Among Greek scholars the Greek of the New Testament was despised as "nonclassical." In point of fact, the difference was exaggerated. There was much variety in the Attic Greek of the great fourth and fifth centuries before Christ. Plato differed from Thucydides, and both differed from the simplicity of Xenophon. Anyone who can read Xenophon can read Luke with no great consciousness of change, and anyone who can read the classically educated writer of the Epistle to the Hebrews could find his way through a book of Herodotus or an oration of Demosthenes without undue frustration. The Common Dialect in which the New Testament was written derived from Attic and was in use four or five centuries later. Nor did everyone in Athens in Pericles' day speak like that great orator.

However, the nonliterary papyri put an end to speculations about "Judaic Greek," "Hebraic Greek," or "the language of the Holy Spirit." Here was Greek "understanded of the people." Luke's opening paragraph demonstrated that he could, if he wished, write in the loftier style of the classical historian; but the vernacular was needed for the transmission of a vital message. In pronunciation there were no doubt differences between Greek as spoken by Romans and Greek as spoken by Alexandrians, but its written form varied little.

J.H. Moulton published the first popular account of the papyri, one of the first steps in the movement that took biblical archaeology out of the university and the scholar's study into the world at large, the newspapers, and to a vast lay public. This book, *From Egyptian Rubbish Heaps*, was published in 1916, just before Camden Cobern published his larger study in America. Moulton's introduction is dated "New Year's Day 1916, Y.M.C.A., Byculla, Bombay." He was in India for a year's missionary work. That he should mention the *Lusitania* in the preface was sadly ironic; for a year later, returning from India, J.H. Moulton died in the Mediterranean, when his ship was torpedoed by a German U-Boat.

Camden Cobern illustrated on a page of his *New Archaeological Discoveries* the wealth of information that came from the one poor little town of Oxyrhynchus. This research showed vividly that not only linguistics benefited from the study of the papyri, but also showed how the life of the people in New Testament times became almost tangible. "The official records and private correspondence in this city," Cobern wrote, "in the first and adjoining centuries are so personal and minute that one almost feels ashamed to repeat some of the disclosures of human frailty and business complications coming from this far-off country town."

Cobern then continued with examples from the first century or thereabouts. A father, in a public notice, accused his son Castor of "riotous living," and proclaimed that he would not be responsible for debts contracted in his name; and another such youth protested to his father against the charge that he was a braggart and was wasting his money on a girl instead of sending it home. Other examples offered concerned the horoscope of a man born at 10 P.M. on September 28, A.D. 15; the hire of a mill, two years later; bail offered for a prisoner in A.D. 28; a guarantee of appearance in court of A.D. 59, and the complaint of a wife against her husband

Women carrying papyrus stalks.

of somewhat earlier date. Syra, the wife, claimed that her husband squandered her dowry, knocked her about, and finally left her without means of support.

One Lois, in A.D. 30, wrote about bread she had ordered that had not been delivered. Perhaps the baker was disturbed by the valuation of his premises, which appeared in another first-century text. A man filed a solemn affidavit that he did not know of any extortion on the part of a soldier mentioned by name. Another document, dated January 31, A.D. 52, is a deed of sale for a donkey. The list could continue almost indefinitely. A woman wrote to her husband telling him she would not even bathe till she heard from him. That was in A.D. 22. A husband wrote to his wife telling her to look after his tools, and mentioning "the old cushion up in the dining room."

The tattered documents bring the common daily life of the New Testament very close to us, and it might be assumed that life in the rest of the Roman world was similar in its humanity to what the common people lived in the valley of the Nile. Apart from the New Testament and the papyri, in only a few odd corners of life are the common people of that time to be seen. There are the remaining chapters of a bawdy novel by Petronius, the elegant senator of Nero's court; the wall scratchings and other fragments recovered from the ruins of Pompeii, sealed for posterity by the ash of Vesuvius; and some recent fragments taken from Qumran and other Dead Sea caves. But these were exceptions. History more often passed the common people by. Ancient documents were usually urban and imperial.

The two volumes of Mikhail I. Rostovtzev, the Russian historian and archaeologist, which appeared in 1926 (*The Economic History of the Roman World*), devoted the first and larger tome to Egypt. The second, half the size, covered the rest of the imperial world. This reflects the mass of the evidence available, thanks to the rainless sands.

2

THE PAPYRI AND THE ROMAN CENSUS

The supreme value of the Eygptian papyri in the study of the New Testament is well illustrated in Luke's account of the birth of Jesus Christ. The third evangelist, a Greek physician probably well-known to the Christian groups of both Antioch and Philippi, linked the story of what happened at Bethlehem to the otherwise unknown first census of the Roman nobleman Quirinius, then governor of Syria. The census of Quirinius during the years A.D. 6-7, mentioned by Luke in his second book (Acts 5:37) and also by Josephus, is well documented. Josephus, the Jewish historian, is accumulating respect as archaeology tests his work.

Luke faces a similar test. He claimed in clear and polished language, the qualities rightly demanded of a true historian: exact reporting, accurate and personal research, the will and diligence to trace major movements and events to their origins, and sound evaluation of eyewitnesses. With such claims calmly made, historians in almost any other sphere might have expected and won a serious hearing. For all the richness of the surviving records of the later decades of the Roman Republic, the first century of the developing autocracy that came to be called the Roman Empire is woefully bereft of contemporary documentation. Apart from a fragmentary inscription from Tibur that might refer to him, little is known of Quirinius himself.

Luke the Historian

Luke was an educated man. He was in possession of vital information concerning a mighty movement of history. While traveling

19

the land during the two years over which Paul was detained in the garrison town of Caesarea, Luke must have become aware that Jesus Christ had moved dramatically into history. Indeed, this was a fact so massively true, as the skeptical Ernest Renan said, that it would be impossible to tear Christ out of history's total fabric without rending its whole structure apart.

Luke quietly affirmed that he was in a better position to tell the full story of the Nativity than anyone else who had sought to compile a record, and he no doubt derived that confidence from the unique opportunity he had to examine eyewitnesses right back "from the beginning" (Luke 1:2). He very likely meant nothing less than an acquaintance with, and a close questioning of, Mary, the mother of Christ, then in the last evening of her life. His first two chapters, delicately written, and with words that had rung for a lifetime in Mary's heart, form a strikingly persuasive tract of literature.

The strange circumstances of the birth of John, the forerunner, were known through all his native hill country. Not so in the case of Mary's son. She had a habit of keeping "things in her heart," pondering and meditating on them. (Luke 2:51). Perhaps Luke was put to some trouble to penetrate these hedges of holy secrecy. But what he was told he recorded, and the central event, if Mary were his source of information, must necessarily rest on the testimony of the woman honored far beyond any other woman of history. Luke, a clearminded man, saw no reason to doubt. But the context of the whole story involved a major act of Roman imperial administration; and Luke's ability to link the doings of one family with the doings of the governing powers, might be very properly tested by the tools and processes of historical investigation. After all, the word *history* derives from a Greek word that means "investigation."

More than any other writer in the New Testament, Luke exposed his narrative to this test. The contribution of archaeology, however, had vindicated triumphantly the historiography of The Acts of the Apostles. That is a matter the most skeptical of critics are constrained to grant. When the same author, with the same quiet assurance, includes in his narrative a miraculous event, scholars like Ernest Renan inhibit their own understanding by a predetermination not to accept what they call miraculous. Such prejudging must be treated patiently and refuted.

Luke must be regarded as a sound historian. He has his place among the Greek writers of history. His first few verses were written in the very manner of the classical historian, as though to honor Theophilus; and then he reverted to the basic simplicity of the common dialect, yet not without charm and a smooth style.

At the turn of the century, William M. Ramsay emerged as the champion of Luke as an exact historian. Classical scholar, historian, and archaeologist, he had a fellowship at Oxford and a professor's chair. He was also Professor of Classics at Aberdeen from 1886 to 1911, the very years when New Testament archaeology and the new study of papyrology were exciting the academic world. Events led him to wide epigraphical studies in Asia Minor, which had the quite unexpected result of changing his whole view of the New Testament. Ramsay went from a vague belief in God to an ardent faith in Christ. Ramsay, in his remarkable book *Was Christ Born at Bethlehem?* first applied the papyrological evidence to the truth of Luke's story of the Roman census at Bethlehem.

Augustus and His Census

The precise date of the census does not matter. I feel fairly convinced the date of the Nativity was in the autumn of 5 B.C. and the census was then two years late. People take too little account of the slow communications of the ancient world. Herod, whose clever family Rome used for a century, would probably avoid taking the census by every legal trick of delay and postponement his wicked, clever mind could devise. We do know that at this time Herod fell out of favor with Augustus and his deep-seated paranoia took root. He could easily have postponed the taking of the census so that 7 B.C. moved on to 5 B.C. before the eminent Quirinius could subdue the highlanders in the central Asia hill country, take overruling powers in Syria, whose governor, Quintilius Varus, Augustus had good reason to distrust, and force the census on Palestine. The

Jews, after David's disastrous census (2 Sam. 24:1-17), detested the whole exercise. Herod was rightly apprehensive.

Augustus, one of the greatest diplomats of all time, is a shadowy person. We do not know him well, but we do know that the preoccupation of his reign was the stabilizing of the frontiers of an Empire. The Northeast, gateway for tribal invasion, was never properly closed, but Augustus did his best, there and elsewhere, to organize the thinly held buffer-lands of which the provinces of Samaria and Judaea were a part. The census during which Christ was born was part of that process.

The Documents

In 1897 three different papyrologists announced almost simultaneously that documents examined by them revealed the Romans in Egypt had established a fourteen year cycle for "enrollments." The same word that appeared in Luke was used. Fragments of the enrollment documents going back to A.D. 20 were discovered. This fell in the correct year of the cycle. A public notice, too, is of supreme interest. It dates from A.D. 104, again a fourteenth year.

Gaius Vibius, chief prefect of Egypt. In view of the approaching census, it is necessary for all those residing for any cause away from their own districts, to prepare to return at once to their own areas of administration, in order that they may meet the family obligation of the enrollment and that the tilled lands may remain in legal possession. Knowing that your district has need of food supplies, I desire...

At this point the document is too tattered to decipher, but the difficulties of logistics and accommodation are implied in the last words. The "inn," or any other lodgings for travelers, would naturally be overwhelmed in the time of an enrollment. But such was the notice which a carpenter named Joseph found posted up in Nazareth one day, and read with a sinking heart. The Roman bureaucrats had little care for the comfort of those whom they ruled, and for census purposes it was convenient to gather the population in their own home towns.

It was probably legally necessary for both Joseph and Mary to present themselves, in accordance with the regulations, in Bethle-

Emperor August
(27 B.C.–A.D. 14).

Bethlehem.

hem. It was no doubt in conformity with a law mentioned twice in the closing chapters of the book of Numbers[1] that Mary had been betrothed to Joseph. Daughters, the law stated, who find themselves heirs to their father's property, must marry within the tribe. Thus Jesus, who was "the son of Mary," of the royal line of David, could only be "King of the Jews" if He were reckoned as the legal son of a member of the same tribe. Hence the genealogy of Joseph in Matthew's Gospel. In Luke's Gospel, Joseph is called "the son of Eli," and this must have been Mary's father, Joseph being considered the legal heir in the absence of sons. This, according to one theory,[2] is the explanation of the variant genealogies in the two Gospels, and it is eminently reasonable.

It may, therefore, have been obligatory for the Holy Family to journey, at that precarious hour, to Bethlehem. Remembering the imperious Roman regulation, some have assumed the presence in the little town of sundry other personalities. Hillel, the great Pharisee, was, it appears, of David's royal line, and in spite of his great age, may have been there that day. And were his son Simeon, and his grandson Gamaliel, at whose feet Paul was to sit, also present? And did this considerable party fill the inn, leaving only the stable for the late arrivals, who had journeyed more tenderly and toilfully?

The next morning Joseph had some documents to file with the authorities. From the Egyptian papyri come many examples of the declarations made by subjects of Rome during the periodic enrollments. The following are two interesting examples. The first dates from A.D. 48, and so is a document of the fourth census after the census mentioned by Luke.

> To Dorian chief magistrate and to Didymus town clerk, from Thermoutharion, the daughter of Thoonis, with her guardian Apollonius the son of Sotades. The inhabitants of the house belonging to me in the South Lane are: Theremoutharion a freedwoman of the aforesaid Sotades, about 65 years of age, of medium height, with honey-colored complexion, having a long face and a scar on the right knee...[A line is missing here which describes a second woman.] I, the aforesaid Thermoutharion [the document continues with an affidavit], with my guardian the said Apollonius, swear by Tiberius Claudius Caesar Emperor, that I have assuredly, honestly and truth-

fully presented the preceding return of those living with me, neither a stranger, Alexandrian, nor freedman, nor Roman, nor Egyptian, except the aforesaid. If I am swearing truly may it be well with me, if falsely the opposite.

The second document is dated something like a century later; and it was chosen because it speaks of a woman who, like Mary (if tradition is correct), must have been a mere girl when her son was born. Tausiris was thirty-four when her son was recorded as aged seventeen.

To Julius Saturnius, officer of the Heracleopolite nome, from Petesouchos son of Pisotis of the village of Ancyronon. I make my return in the 9th year of Antoninus Caesar, the lord, in accordance with the order of Valerius Proclus the prefect. Myself, Petesouchos aged 42, my wife Tausiris daughter of Pareitis, aged 34, Pnephorus my son aged 17. I swear by the fortune of the emperor that I have presented the aforesaid return honestly and truthfully and have told no lie nor omitted anyone who ought to have been returned by me, nor taken an advantage of identity of names. Otherwise may I endure the consequences of the oath.

Joseph would have had another document to submit for the satisfaction of a bureaucratic age. This was a notification of birth. Many of these documents survive, and the one chosen speaks of a young mother with a husband very considerably older than herself. It dates from the year A.D. 150.

To Socrates and Didymus scribes of the metropolis from Ischyras son of Protas son of Mysthes, his mother being Tasoucharion, daughter of Didas, of the district of Hermonthrace, and from his wife Thiasarion, daughter of Ammonius, son of Mysthes of the same district. We register the son who was born to us, Ischyras, being one year of age in the present year, the 14th, of Antoninus Caesar the lord. I therefore present this notification of birth. Ischyras, aged 44, without distinguishing marks. Thiasarion, aged 24 without distinguishing marks. Written for them by Ammonius, public scribe.

A second registration of birth dated exactly a century earlier, in A.D. 50, might be added.

To Arius son of Lysimachus, village scribe of Tebtunis, from Psoiphis son of Harpocras son of Pakebkis, his mother being Thenmarsisuchus daughter of Psoithis and Kellauthis, inhabitants of the village, priest of the fifth tribe of the gods at the village, Cronos, the most great god, and Isis and Sarapis, the great gods, and one of the fifty exempted persons. I register Pakebkis, the son born to me and Taasies daughter of...and Taopis in the 10th year of Tiberius Claudius Caesar Augustus Germanicus Imperator, and request that the name of my aforesaid son Pakebkis be entered on the list...

The papyrus is mutilated but the above gives the general sense. Psoiphis was "exempted" presumably from taxes, as a priest in office. The boy was "entered on the list" as an aspirant for the priesthood. The father of John the Baptist might have completed a similar document.

The Enrollment—An Historian's Note

These ancient documents of officialdom will suggest the atmosphere of Bethlehem on the night of the Nativity. As the returning people of the town sat around David's Well to renew old acquaintance and exchange tales of life abroad, there would be much fierce talk of Rome. Palestine was a turbulent province, and in many hearts smoldered that fierce resentment which blazed out sixty years later into the fire and passion of the Great Rebellion—a savage and hopeless struggle against the might of the Empire, which ended only with the destruction of Jerusalem, and the decimation of a race. Christ was born in occupied territory and anyone who would understand what men were thinking in the world to which He came must take that fact into account. Men and women have not changed essentially in two thousand years, and the bitter experience of alien rule was a commonplace of life in the world of the first century. "O little town of Bethlehem," runs the carol, "how still we see thee lie." Bethlehem was anything but quiet on that crowded night.

These documents have something more than human interest. William Ramsay, convinced by his studies in the Acts of the Apostles that Luke the evangelist was an historian of first-rate integrity and accuracy, set out to establish the historical truth of the complex of events surrounding the Nativity.

> "Obviously," he wrote in his book *Was Christ Born at Bethlehem?*, "the story of Luke One and Two can never be demonstrated. There will always remain a large step to be taken in faith.... But it is highly important to show that the circumstances with which Luke connects this marvelous event are true, and that, in things which can be tested, he does not fall below the standard of accuracy demanded of ordinary historians."[3]

This Ramsay proceeded to do. The decree which illustrates the obligation under which the Holy Family found themselves to proceed to their ancestral hometown of Bethlehem, has already been quoted. Ramsay made use of the enrollment returns to establish the fourteen-year rhythm of the Roman census, and to show that an enrollment took place in Palestine between the years 9 and 6 B.C..

The historical attestation for an earlier governorship of Quirinius in Syria in 5 B.C. remains a problem, and is not one which archaeology can presently solve. Inscriptions, nonetheless, may locate Quirinius in office in Syria and Cilicia during the vital years and offer a framework of conjecture into which Luke's story can convincingly fit. The matter is outside our present theme. Those curious to follow the argument which plausibly dates the birth of Christ in the autumn of 5 B.C. may find it set out in an appendix to *The Century of the New Testament*.[4]

NOTES

[1] Numbers 27:1-11; 36:1-13. (See J. N. Geldenhuys, *Commentary On The Gospel Of Luke*, pp. 150-155.)

[2] For another suggestion see J. Gresham Machen, *The Virgin Birth Of Christ*, pp. 203 sqq.

[3] Op. cit., pp. 112, 113.

[4] Pp. 147-151. By E. M. Blaiklock (Tyndale Press).

3

THE PAPYRI AND THE WORDS OF
CHRIST

Archaeology has hardly anything to say on the physical appearance of the Lord. The spurious letter of Publius Lentulus, though it may remotely perpetrate an ancient tradition, is no more than fourteenth century fiction. The rough art of the Catacombs, where Jesus is shown in various contexts, predominantly as the Good Shepherd, reveals a beardless young man, and as far as such simple graffiti can convey an impression, gentle and benign in facial expression. There are said to have been statues of Christ in Jerash and Caesarea. If there were, the former may have been Aesculapius, the latter Hadrian. A mosaic likeness from the Catacomb of Saint Callixtus dates from the fourth century, and another, from the same time or a little later, was found on a villa site at Hinton Saint-Mary in Dorset. Mosaic, however, is a notably poor medium for the representation of detailed physical characteristics.

There is no ancient written description of Jesus. From a few contexts the power of his eyes might be glimpsed. He "looked up" when the poor woman slipped her tiny contribution into the temple treasury (Luke 21:1-4). He looked up when they challenged him over the stricken woman in the courtyard (John 7:53-8:11). At His look the accusers hesitated, as did the armed squad about to arrest Him in the garden on the betrayal night (John 18:1-8).

Instead of statues or paintings, the words of Christ reveal Him to us, and the papyri have much that is useful to know. They cast a bright light on the background of much that He said. Of that,

29

something will be said in the following chapter. Let us first look at the so-called *logia* and examine them for the realities of Christ.

Ernest Renan, the French Hebraist of the last century, had a remarkable perception of the power of Christ's recorded words.

> A sort of glitter at once mild and terrible, a divine force, if I may so speak, underlines these words, detaches them from the context and makes them easily distinguishable. Anyone who takes up the task of carving a consecutive narrative out of evangelical history, has here an excellent touchstone. The actual words of Jesus reveal themselves...we feel them vibrate. They translate themselves spontaneously and fit naturally into the narrative.[1]

This should be the guiding rule, when we are confronted in the papyri with sayings of Christ and seek to assess their authenticity and value today.

The Sayings of Christ

We have it on John's authority that Jesus said many things that were not recorded (John 21:25). Paul quoted one such statement: "It is more blessed to give than to receive" (Acts 20:35). Clement of Alexandria, born in A.D. 150, preserved three sayings, two of which seem to bear the test of which Renan wrote: "Ask great things and the small shall be added to you," and "Be honest money changers." When one bears in mind that in all the eighteen centuries between us and Clement there scarcely appeared one saying in each generation to compare with the golden words of Christ, it is remarkable to find the emergence of words that rigorous scrutiny is constrained to pass as genuine.

Two statements with a flavor of authenticity were preserved by Moslems. The poet, Nizami, wrote how Jesus came into a crowded market place one evening. An idle crowd was gathered in a corner looking at an object of gruesome interest. Coming up behind them unobserved the Lord saw a dead dog. Dogs did not fare well in ancient regard. They were a metaphor for loathing and disgust. The "evil men from the market place" such as those to whom Luke refers in his story of Thessalonica (KJV's "lewd fellows of the baser sort," Acts 17:5), were remarking on the dead creature's

30

bare ribs, torn hide and ragged ears. A frayed and filthy rope was round its neck. Jesus, unobserved, stood listening to their obscene comments. Quietly He said: "Pearls cannot rival the whiteness of his teeth." Men turned, startled and rebuked. "This must be Jesus of Nazareth," one said. He had a way of saying words that burned the heart and quenched evil. "He who is without sin among you, let him throw a stone at her first" (John 8:7), was such a statement. He waited, writing something with His finger in the sand on the flagstones. The accusers, their spirits stripped bare before Him, dropped their stones and slipped away.

In a town twenty-four miles west of Agra is a big mosque with a magnificent gateway 120 feet high and broad. In the scrolled decorations of doorposts and plinth an Arabic sentence is written. "Jesus, on whom be peace, said, 'The world is merely a bridge, you are to pass over it, and not to build your dwellings upon it.' " How has the saying come to the Indian mosque? There is a tradition, so strong as to be certainly true, that Thomas and Bartholomew preached the gospel in India. There is a strong and ancient branch of the Indian church that antedates modern missionary enterprise.

This Christian community Akbar founded when he took up the reins of India. Akbar was an enlightened Moslem. Like the Roman Emperor Severus, who had statues of Abraham, Christ, and Orpheus in his private chapel, Akbar tried to fuse the religions of his realm and even invited a Portuguese missionary from Goa to preach there. The saying of Christ over a mosque that Akbar founded is a relic of this enlightened policy.

What did the saying mean? The only river in Palestine is the Jordan, and it was crossed not by bridges but by fords. Where did the Lord, who always linked His teaching to known, familiar things, see a bridge? As recorded in the Gospels, He once preached at Tyre. Tyre in those days was a sorry ruin of the mighty commercial city of the Phoenicians who held Cyprus, founded Carthage, sent ships to India and Britain, and supplied the master-builders with the great cedar beams for Solomon's temple in Jerusalem. Tyre was an island until, more than three centuries before Christ, Alexander of Macedon came. In the pride of her strength Tyre closed her gates and bade the Greek do his worst.

Alexander responded with his usual dynamic energy. He built a causeway across the water, took his engines and assault troops across to the walls, and stormed the city. The causeway, widened by the drifting sands to a full quarter of a mile, still exists. In Christ's day it had the appearance of a bridge. Was it in this connection that Christ uttered His words? The causeway of Tyre was a road. No one, as on old London Bridge, built houses on it. Like Abraham, we look "for the city which has foundations" (Heb. 10:11). In search of it, we wander like nomads.

Another example of a lost saying came from Theodore Beza, a French Calvinist, who lived from 1519 to 1605. Beza published a Greek and Latin text of the New Testament in 1565. It was given in 1581 to the University of Cambridge and it was probably of fifth century origin. It contains a few peculiarities, especially a saying of Christ, slipped into Luke's text. The saying went" "On the same day he saw someone working on the Sabbath. He said: 'Man, if you know what you are doing you are to be counted happy. If not you are under a curse and are a transgressor of the Law.' " Whether this is genuine, it is hard to say. The meaning is that a man is to be congratulated if he has grasped the truth that the law was being superseded by a new order, and that the Sabbath was made for man and was not the burden on life that legalists had made it. If he was deliberately disobeying the law from a base motive, he fell under the sanctions of the law.

There were many collections of such sayings. According to strong tradition, Matthew's gospel itself was, in its first form, an Aramaic collection of Christ's sayings. The final form in Greek, as might be seen in any Bible, abounds in Christ's words, including the Sermon on the Mount. Confirmation of this came from odd quarters. In his spirited history of the Crusade of Louis IX of France, or Saint Louis as he came to be called (1248 to 1254), Jean De Joinville of Champagne told of the embassage of Brother Yves, a Breton monk, to "the Old Man of the Mountain." This villain's keep was high in the Lebanon ranges, still visible in jagged ruin from the Golan heights. The Old Man had a "hit team." He doped his band of desperadoes with Indian hemp, hashish or marijuana, and sent them out on assassination missions. They were called hashish men, or *hashishin*, whence, of course, "assassins."

Brother Yves was sent by Louis to assess the situation. He found the ancient scoundrel was in possession of a book called "the words of the Lord to Peter," but unfortunately failed to secure a copy. He did, however, commend the Old Man for his bedside reading. It might, of course, have been a copy of Mark's Gospel of which the substance was given, says tradition, by Peter to Mark. It might have been, on the other hand, a collection of sayings otherwise unknown, like those discovered in 1945 in earthenware containers, such as held the Dead Sea Scrolls.

This is the story. Digging on the site of a fourth-century monastery, at Nag Hammadi between Cairo and Luxor, some peasants found a large jar of papyri. The fact that its contents at last reached the West, in the midst of the Suez crisis in 1956, was due to the Belgian scholar, Gilles Quispel. It was his enterprise and patience that at last brought the discovery through the lamentable black market in antiquities and persuaded the jealous Moslem librarians

The Nag Hammadi codices.

A leaf from the Gospel of Truth, *a Nag Hammadi codex.*

of Egypt to release the precious information so reprehensibly withheld for fourteen years.

The major "treasure in earthen vessels," to use Paul's phrase (2 Cor. 4:7), was the so-called *Gospel of Thomas*, some inkling of which had been seen in one of the documents found by Bernard Grenfell and Arthur Hunt in 1903. There were 114 sayings of Christ, isolated words or brief conversations, some known, some quite unknown. Some are most obviously spurious, and fall far short of Renan's guidelines, having none of that edge and aura so characteristic of the New Testament. Others are fresh and pungent and might be genuine. For example, "Whoever is near to me is near the fire, and whoever is far from me is far from the kingdom." Origen, the Greek church father whose main activity lay in the first half of the third century, had quoted the first part of this saying. It was a warning of the persecution and pain which true discipleship can often cost.

Consider, too, the words "become passers-by" quoted from the Indian mosque. The words in no way commend the shirking of duty that marked the priest and the Levite on the Jericho road (Luke 10:30-37), but complement the words already mentioned. "The world is a bridge."

It is natural enough that some of these sayings in the *Gospel of Thomas* present a slightly worn appearance, for the writing is dated about A.D. 140, almost half a century after John closed the canon of the New Testament. Compare for example, the well-known parable of the sower and the seed with this slightly blurred and attenuated version.

> See, the sower went out, he filled his hand, he threw. Some seed fell on the road, the birds came, they gathered them. Others fell on the rock, and did not strike root in the earth, and did not produce ears. And others fell on the thorns. They choked the seed and the worm ate them. And others fell on the good earth, and brought forth good fruit. It bore sixty per measure, and one hundred and twenty per measure.

The closing words are a little obscure, but note the Semitic method of counting.

These sayings are obviously from a different tradition, held, no doubt, by the Christian community that escaped from Jerusalem before its fall in A.D. 70, and quite independent of that so richly represented in the Gospels. It is a remarkable testimony to the trustworthiness of the Bible.

As a footnote consider the pungent little parable of the woman with the cracked jar. It is a Nag Hammadi comment on some of the pseudo-theologies of our day.

> The Kingdom of the Father is like a woman who was carrying a jar full of meal. While she was walking on a distant road the handle of the jar broke. The meal streamed out behind her on the road. She did not know it. She had noticed no accident. After she came into her house, she put the jar down and found it empty.

To carry the Bread of Life in a modern container is a fine idea, but we must be sure that the container is such that the contents are not lost.

The Oxyrhynchus Papyri

It is not surprising, therefore, that a community so strong in Christian tradition as Oxyrhynchus should leave among its records some fragmented sheets of Christ's sayings. Among the material discovered there was a Christian hymn with the musical notation complete, the first Christian music ever found. Grenfell and Hunt began working there in 1896 and almost immediately found the first sheet of sayings. It was published the next year.

Consider the following: "I stood in the midst of the world and was visible to men...my soul grieves over the sons of men, because they are blind in their hearts." The infinite pathos of the words matches the lament over Jerusalem (Matt. 23:37). And there is a mysterious remark: "Whenever there are two they are not without God, and wherever there is one alone I am with him. Raise the stone and there you will find me. Split the wood and there I am." The word to the lonely is plain enough, but is the second half of the saying continuous or separate? Loneliness is not a matter of numbers. A man can be lonely in a crowd. There are the "despised and rejected by men" (Is. 53:3). The Lord Himself was lonely. Did Christ mean that the makers of roads, the woodcutters and water carriers (Josh. 9:21), were not beyond His knowledge, His presence and His care? The meaning of such sayings need not be limited. This one takes place among the world's wise words.

A second sheet of sayings came to light from the same source in February, 1903. It was, as the excavators of the site said, "a curious stroke of good fortune." Publication was again a year later. One saying stands out: "Let him who seeks cease not till he finds, and when he finds he will be astonished, astonished he shall reach the Kingdom and there he shall rest." It should be remembered that the imperatives in the Greek of the Sermon on the Mount are in a linear or continuous tense called "the present." Consequently they contain no promise of instant discovery. It is a case of "keep on seeking, keep on knocking" (Matt. 7:7).

Astonishment means wonder. Wonder is the very first step in knowledge, as the greatest of Greek philosophers, Plato, said. Wonder is the base of all man's tireless examination of his environment. This is true in the spiritual as well as in the scientific field. The mind that does not wonder is dead. As Elizabeth Browning's poem put it, every common bush is "ablaze with God." The rest "sit round it and pick blackberries." Wonder is the mark of the questing soul who treads the highway to truth, and astonishment is the thrill of continual discovery.

Apart, of course, from these nonbiblical sayings, there are multitudes of fragments of the New Testament, some going back to the second century. Perhaps when the latest shreds from Qumran are evaluated it may be possible to push the record back into the first century. Reconstructing a complete text of the New Testament from fragments of papyrus up to the fifth cenury is possible; back that is, to the death of Augustine and the fall of the western Roman Empire. Thus it is possible to say that the original text of the New Testament is fixed as certainly as are Shakespeare's plays, though, admittedly, that is not a contribution of papyrology alone.

Conclusions

No serious historian would question the historicity of Jesus Christ. He is part of the woven fabric of man's history. So much for the central fact, however much critical minds might contest recorded details. The words of Jesus, nonetheless, from Matthew's account of the Sermon on the Mount to John's summary of the discourses of the betrayal night, are alone evidence enough for the appearance in history of a most extraordinary person. To their total the papyri added a few sentences with the authentic ring of the New Testament about them. In any dictionary of quotations the sayings of Christ, from the first book of the New Testament alone, would outnumber the selected quotations from all the surviving writers of the century in which he lived, a surprisingly small group, to be sure, but including authors of sententious power like Tacitus and Juvenal.

The *logia*, or sayings, which have come to view since 1896, belong to a continuing tradition. More than that, they reveal, on the negative side, the complete futility of misguided attempts outside that mainstream to add to or expand the crisp penetrating language of the original records of the apostolic band. Along with second-century legend-making and romancing about Christ in the apocryphal narratives, the logia underline the purity of the evangelical records.

Some papyri reinforce what stands recorded. We have seen a few papyri emerge from nineteen centuries of obscurity to stand the stern test of comparison. In their mass they show that Christ lived, and, dying at the age of thirty-three, left in remembered speech such authority that men sought its cover and support. Much of the ancient record is still an open story, as the fragment from the New South Wales University from the Acts of the Apostles shows. The Qumran caves have added bits to the collection of first century records in the last dozen years. Possibly, there are more papyrus discoveries to make. Truth, more truth, as Psalm 85 says, may yet "spring out of the earth" (Ps. 85:11).

NOTE

[1] Joseph Ernest Renan. *Life of Christ* [1864].

4

THE PAPYRI AND THE PARABLES

The documents of daily life recovered from Egypt illuminate and bring close the details of the New Testament that are enshrined a little remotely in the book itself. "Do not lay up for yourselves treasures on earth," said Christ on the hill above the fishers' bays, "where moth and rust destroy and where thieves break in and steal" (Matt. 6:19). The words are clear enough and even remind the modern reader that the ancient burglar dug through the plaster walls or the mud-brick mixed with straw. But how vividly this little petition of Euhemeria of the Arsinoite district in Egypt brings the tragic situation of personal loss and injury to life:

> To Lysanias, chief officer of the Arsinoite ward from Artemidorus son of Irenaeus. On the night before the 22nd of Pharmouthi of the present 20th year of Tiberius certain persons raided the land and farm owned by Marcus Apollonius Saturninus near Euhemeria, and carried off on donkey-back 30 bundles of hay from three hectares of land. I therefore file this report so that the chief of the area police may look into it, and that the culprits may be brought before you for proper penalty.
> Farewell.

The date places this sad little complaint in the same decade as the Sermon on the Mount. There is a similar complaint about the stripping of some olive trees from the same area from two years earlier.

The Parables

Such glimpses of common life are best associated with the parables of Christ, which are tales of the ordinary folk who have been passed by in the writings of the great poets, philosophers, historians, and satirists of the first century. Only the novel the *Satiricon* by Petronius, a contemporary of Nero, gives a glimpse of them; and the actors in its bawdy tale are disgusting scamps, hardly typical of the common people of the parables.

There is no story in literature so shaped to reveal the wickedness of mankind as the story of Herod Antipas and John the Baptist (Mark 6:14-29). But evil and petty sin are not the monopoly of a Herod or a Pilate, as the powerful stories Christ told abundantly reveal. The papyri provide the richest illustration. Consider for a first example the tale of the Prodigal Son.

The Gospels are not rigidly ordered chronological narratives, but it does appear that Christ was teaching in Galilee on His last slow progress from the days of rest at Caesarea Philippi to Jerusalem and the Passion. Galilee was a farmland on rolling hills. The lake, a long blue basin in the Jordan Rift, six hundred feet below the level of the sea, divides Galilee from the crowded Decapolis beyond the Golan Heights that wall the east of the lake. Those ten towns, which the name reflects, were mainly Greek, from Damascus, the most Jewish among them, to Amman, the ancient Philadelphia. There was abundant contact across and around the water between Jews and Greeks. Indeed, Bethshan, to use the old name, was one of the ten towns, and lay on the Jewish side of Jordan.

The city of Gerasa retains some flavor of that vanished world. It is a large and extensive ruin, not lost, as are Damascus and Amman, under the mass of contemporary building. Gerasa, modern Jerash, is one of the most imposing archaeological sites of the ancient world. It has an oval forum completely ringed with pillars and a high-lifted theater that enable the audience on the stone seats to look over the heads of the actors into a long and lovely boulevard of tall temples, houses, and shops. These buildings stand as a stone memorial to the city where perhaps the Prodigal Son from Galilee could have come on foot in a few days. He went "to a far country, and there wasted his possessions with prodigal living" (Luke 15:13). The region of Gerasa was a country far enough, if its common way of life was set beside the quiet dignity of the old-fashioned household in Galilee.

Gerasa (Jerash).

Some itinerant Greek sophist, perhaps, had persuaded the lad that nothing could be known that the senses could not tell us; obviously life is physical experience; and Gerasa offered a young man scope and opportunity. What he did not tell him was that the capacity of the body is limited, and by weaving words philosophy can argue itself out of argument. The same Greek might then have aided his cynical townsmen to fleece the gullible country boy of his money and property.

Meanwhile the father waited. The view is wide from the Galilean uplands above the Jordan Valley. The upper end of the fertile river plain is visible as patches of brown, green, and gold. The river, a blue sinuous line, winds south. The lake is a level floor to the east and north. The father often watched the road winding down the hill to the river. And one day he saw his son limping home in rags "and ran and fell on his neck and kissed him" (Luke 15:20). The wait was over, but not the pain. There was an elder brother, meticulous in conduct, but merciless, jealous, and without any understanding of his father's mercy. The elder brother's spiritual blindness was like that of the Pharisees whom Christ criticized. In Gerasa's oval forum where the Pharisees might debate, they knew all the rules of religion, every subtle detail of the law, but knew little mercy for the outcast, the underprivileged, and the alien.

A papyrus of the turn of the first century provides some background. It was first published by Adolf Deissmann, still considered a pioneer in papyrology in spite of some erroneous linguistic conclusions. The papyrus is a letter from a son to his mother.

Antonis Longus to Nilous, his mother, many greetings. I always pray for your health. I had no hope that you would come up to town. That is why I did no go there. I was ashamed to come for I am going round in rags. I beg you, mother, forgive me. I know that I have brought it upon myself. I have been punished, in any case. I know that I have sinned.

The letter continues with blame for a friend named Postumus, who seems to have told Nilous about her prodigal son, but the papyrus is too illegible to be read satisfactorily.

There were other fathers who killed no fatted calf (the adjective, by the way, is applied to a bird in a papyrus of A.D. 1). A story of an Assyrian father was well known as a popular folktale in the Middle East. It was written before 500 B.C. and a tattered papyrus containing part of the text was discovered in Egypt during excavations at Elephantine in 1906 or a little later. Ahikar, a high official of Sennacherib, was wronged by his adoptive son, Nadan. When oppurtunity came, he put the boy in chains, gave him a thousand blows on the shoulders, and as many on the loins. The boy pleaded for forgiveness saying he was no more worthy to be called a son, but would gladly feed the pigs. To this the father replied: "To him who does good, good shall be rendered. To him that does evil, evil shall be rewarded." Perhaps this tale was known in the first century because in a Syriac version of the New Testament some copyist or translator of Luke makes the Prodigal say: "Forgive this folly. I will feed the pigs that are in your house." There would, of course, be no pigs in that Jewish home.

Some fathers would approve of Ahikar, rather than of the godly old man of the Lord's story. A public notice from the first or second century serves as an example.

> To Heracleides, ruler of the Hermapolite ward from Ammonius the elder, the son of Ermaeus, and his former wife A...along with her present husband Callistratus...Since our son Castor, along with others, by riotous living has squandered all his own property, and now has laid hands on ours and desires to scatter it, on that account we are taking precautions lest he should deal despitefully with us or do anything else amiss...We beg therefore that a proclamation be set up [that no one should lend him money].

There are many such documents among the papyri, some of them almost savage in their expression of deep resentment against wayward children. The following, for example, is part of a deed of disownment in which a father cast off two sons and two daughters.

> Thinking to find you a comfort to my age, submissive and obedient, you in your prime have set yourselves against me like rancorous beings. Wherefore I reject and abhor you...

The document runs on with legal abuse for some five hundred words. If the papyri are any indication, the father who killed the fatted calf for his lost boy's returning was gracious beyond custom of that ancient world.

Catalogue of Scamps

There is a second story that Luke discovered in his two years of wandering in the land and included in his unique central group of parables. "So the master commended the unjust steward" (Luke 16:8), the small story of cheating ends, because he had acted wisely. The "lord," of course, was the landlord not Christ. He was the scamp's employer and a jolly fellow. Rich enough to laugh at the loss of a few payments of wine and oil, he expressed a rueful praise for the simple way his "unjust steward" had contrived to extricate himself from his immediate predicament.

The parable's point is that the rogues of the world will leave no stone unturned to gain their end. The world will watch and grimly praise them, as they turn the world's resources to their purpose. But what of this enterprise in a nobler sphere? Cannot Christians scheme as indefatigably for the kingdom's sake? "Make friends for yourselves," the Lord concluded, "by unrighteous mammon" (Luke 16:9). If rascals can use money to build themselves comfort, cannot others use it for God?

From the Egyptian papyri a band of scoundrels in office can be assembled. It was a highly regimented age. In Egypt an ancient fiscal system had been taken over by the Greeks, and then the Romans, producing taxation and governmental controls modern in their complexity. Documents, reports, statements, deeds, receipts, and all the paraphernalia of business and bureaucracy were part of Egypt's way of life. Here are three examples.

The first is a complaint of petty theft on a demolition job, dated from the year of the crucifixion and resurrection of Christ.

To Serapion, chief of police, from Orsenouphis son of Harpaesis, notable of the village of Euhemeria in the division of Themistes. In the month Mesore of the past 14th year of Tiberius Caesar I was having some old walls on my premises demolished by the mason Petesouchus, son of Petesouchus, and while I was absent from home to gain my living, Petesouchus, in the process of demolition, discovered a hoard which had been secreted by my mother in a little box as long ago as the 16th year of Augustus Caesar, consisting of a pair of gold earrings weighing 4 quarters, a gold crescent weighing 3 quarters, a pair of silver armlets of the weight of 12 drachmae of uncoined metal, a necklace with silver ornaments worth 80 drachmae, and 60 silver drachmae. Diverting the attention of his assistants and my people, he had them conveyed to his own home by his maiden daughter, and after emptying out the aforesaid objects he threw away the box empty in my house, and he even admitted finding the box, though he pretends that it was empty. Wherefore I request, if you approve, that the accused be brought before you for the consequent punishment. Farewell.

Orsenouphis, aged 50, scar on left forearm.

A futher illustration of the documentary preoccupation of that paper-ridden age is a deed of apprenticeship to a weaver dated A.D. 183. Like the lease for the papyrus swamp mentioned in chapter 1, it shows the detail into which people went to insure against cheating and corruption.

Tryphon son of Dionysius son of Tryphon and of Thamounis daughter of Onnophris, and Ptolemaeus son of Pausirion son of Ptolemaeus and of Ophelous daughter of Theon, weaver, both being inhabitants of Oxyrhynchus, mutually acknowledge that Tryphon had apprenticed to Ptolemaeus his son Thoonis, whose mother is Saraeus daughter of Apion, and who is not yet of age, for a period of one year from the present day, to serve and to follow all the instructions given to him by Ptolemaeus in the art of weaving as far as he himself knows it, the boy to be fed and clothed for the whole period by his father Tryphon, who will also be responsible for all taxes on him, on the condition that Ptolemaeus will pay to him monthly on account of food 5 drachmae and at the close of the whole period on account of clothing 12 drachma, nor shall Tryphon have the right to remove the boy from Ptolemaeus until the completion of the period, and for whatever days therein the boy plays truant, he shall send him to work for the like number at the end of it, or else forfeit one drachma of silver for each day, and for removing him within the period he shall pay a penalty of 100 drachma and the like sum to the Treasury. If Ptolemaeus fails to instruct the boy fully, he shall be liable to the same penalties. This contract of apprenticeship is valid. The 13th year of Nero Claudius Caesar Augustus Germanicus Imperator, the 21st of the month Sebastus. [Signed] I, Ptolemaeus son of Pausirion son of Ptolemaeus and of Ophelous daughter of Theon, will do everything in the one year. I, Zoilus son of Horus son of Zoilus and of Dieus daughter of Sokeus have written for him, as he is illiterate. The 13th year of Nero Claudius Caesar Imperator, Sebastus 21.

It is a comment on human nature that such societies produce graft and offer unbounded opportunities for the nefarious activities of such scoundrels as the unjust steward and the tax collectors of the Gospels. One such man is known to the modern world from a letter file discovered by Grenfell and Hunt in a crocodile cemetery at Tebtunis. The crocodile was sacred in Egypt, and on demise received honorable burial. Sick of finding the dry carcasses where he had hoped for sarcophagi and baksheesh, a workman smashed one open with his pick and revealed that it was stuffed with waste papyri. Most of the documents were official records, and Menches' note was among them.

> On being appointed to the post of town clerk, I will pay at the village 50 measures of wheat, and 50 measures of pulse, namely, 20 of lentils and 10 of bruised beans, 6 of mixed seed, 10 of peas, 3 of mustard and 1 of parched pulse: total 100 measures.

The office he sought was honorary. He offered payment and his letter mentioned no recipient and bore no date. Menches' undertaking to cultivate certain land is also mentioned in a document in his file. It is dated 119 B.C..

> Asclepiades to Marres greeting. Menches having been appointed by the dioecetes to the village secretaryship of Kerkeosiris on the understanding that he shall cultivate at his own expense fifteen hectares of the land in the area of the village which has been reported as unproductive, at a rent of fifty measures, to the Government in full, or else make up the deficiency from his private means, give to him the papers of his office and take care that the terms of his undertaking are fulfilled. Goodbye. Year 51, Mesore 3. [Addressed] To Marres, district secretary.

Why was Menches so eager to hold his petty office? Simpler men were eager to escape the honorary burden. We might read, for example, the appeal of a doctor who found himself saddled with a local magistracy.

> After toiling for four years at my post, I am become very run down, my lord. I entreat you, my preserver, have pity, and order me to be released from my duties. Add instructions, please, that those practicing medicine be granted exemption, especially those who, like myself, have passed the examinations.

Why then did Menches want the post? Reading between the lines in the private letters of the age we gather that an official could often turn a shady drachma. Consider this letter of A.D. 200:

Ammonius to Apion, greetings. If you can, buy up all the peaches on the market. Don't neglect it, for if the gods will, the government is about to market them. Don't be fainthearted. Manage this so that peaches can be bought through you alone, and know that you will not suffer as far as I am concerned.

What is probably the first mention of peaches in all literature, introduces us to a bureaucratic marketing scheme to corner the crop. It was an advantage to Apion to have a friend like Ammonius in an official position.

Menches might have looked for more than inside information on marketing legislation. All the village taxes would pass through his hands. He would be registrar, too, of all trades and properties. "A certain Artemidorus, scribe of Ciris," complained a lady named Seniphibis, "has registered me as having more land than I possess, and in consequence inflicts much loss on me." "The collection of grain dues," complained another, in A.D. 215, "is based on obsolete lists of names, and the collections are involving injustice to many." Both documents give us a glimpse of a thoroughly corrupt bureaucracy. Menches, too, would deal with all applications for rent rebates. A burning question, as early as the first century, was the just rate of rebate for government tenants in years when the flooding of the Nile proved disappointing. The bureaucrats seem never to have succeeded in establishing a workable sliding scale. Tiberius Julius Alexander, Governor of Egypt in the late first century, condemned the practice of basing rents on a past average, but as late as Hadrian we find the problem still worrying officialdom. In both Greek and Roman times everything one did or ate in Egypt was taxed. Hermaiscus opened a vegetable shop in Broad Street at Pson in A.D. 222, and we have the receipt for his registration fee. All the other shops in Broad Street, and every trade, suffered like infliction. It even cost a handful of good drachma to die, for there was a tax on grave digging. There must have been pickings for men like Menches, if they "walked on their feet in the market place," to use the quaint term that appears in declarations of testamentary capacity.

It must have been annoying for a painter to have Menches assess his canvas, for, oddly enough, there was a tax on paintings. What an opportunity to levy taxes when a grandee passed through on the way to the pyramids. His food and transport would be taxed in the process. It was well for the farmer next door to be the town clerk's friend, even at the expense of "31 dishes and one meal bowl," which Pachon took to the pawnshop on "the 10th" of an undecipherable month and year.

A letter from Menches' own decade, dated 112 B.C., must have made the petty official who received it groan. The end of the letter is too mutilated to read the list of "gifts mentioned below." It might also be noted that Petesouchus was a crocodile-god and that the Labyrinth was the temple beside the pyramid of Amenemhet III at Hawara.

> Hermias to Horus greeting. Below is a copy of the letter to Ascle-piades. Take care then that instructions are followed. Goodbye. Year 5, Xandious 17, Mecheir 17.
> To Asclepiades. Lucius Memmius, a Roman senator, who occupies a position of great dignity and honor, is sailing up from Alexandria to the Arsinoite ward to see the sights. Let him be received with special magnificence, and take care that at the proper spots the guest-chambers be prepared and the landing-places to them be completed, and that the furniture of the guest-chamber, the tidbits for Petesouchus the crocodile spirit and the crocodiles, the conveniences for viewing the Labyrinth, and the offerings and sacrifices be provided. In general take the greatest pains in everything to see that the visitor is satisfied, and display the utmost zeal.

The accounts, of course, were audited. But what then? A letter from Menches' hoard reads: "Polemon to Menches, greeting. The inspector from the Treasury will pass your village on the 16th, so try to have all arrears in order." Another official wrote: "The inspector of temple finance is here. Write up your books and come to me, for he is a very stern fellow. If anything detains you, send them on and I will see you through, for he has become my friend."

5

ARCHAEOLOGY AND CHRIST'S DEATH

Archaeology has much to say on the events of Passion Week, a week that changed the course of human history.

John's Gospel, especially, reveals that the Lord had long anticipated His trial and crucifixion and knew that His path lay through that last encounter with evil. In the fine archaeological museum at Athens is a remarkable large bas-relief from Eleusis, which few seem to have realized comes to vivid life in the light of a strange conversation of Christ recorded in John's gospel.

Some Greeks had come to see Christ. These Greeks were not Jews of the Dispersion in the great Greek world, who were sometimes contemptuously referred to as "Greeks" by the metropolitan Jewry, but were ethnic Greeks, probably from the trans-Jordanian Decapolis. The Decapolis was an area extending from Damascus and the Golan plateau to Philadelphia, which is today Amman, the capital of Jordan. This area might have housed a million Greeks and fronted Galilee across the seven-mile-wide basin of the Lake Galilee. Geresa was one of the ten city centers, and its great ruins lie in today's Jerash, which we have suggested was the "far country" of the Prodigal's wanderings. Since Christ had crossed the lake and ordained the first apostle to the Gentiles there, the maniac He had cured at Gadara, it was possible that questing Greeks already knew about Him. "Sir," said the polite visitors to Andrew, "we wish to see Jesus." And He made a curious comment to the visitors. "Unless a grain of wheat falls into the ground and dies, it remains alone; but if it dies, it produces much grain" (John 12:21-24).

The Demeter Myth and Eleusis

Hence the curious relevance of the tall slab of carved stone in the archaeological museum. It was carved in the fifth century before Christ and most probably stood in the temple at Eleusis where a religious cult very dear to the Athenians was housed. Eleusis is today an industrial suburb of Athens; but in Athens' great fifth century it was a rural and maritime suburb that had once been a tiny king-

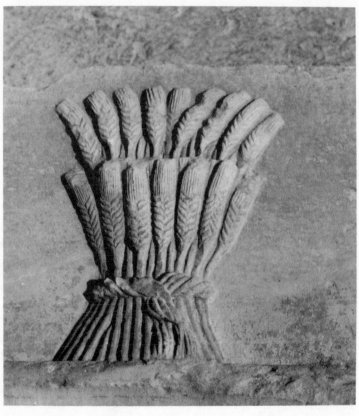

A sheaf of wheat from Eleusis.

dom, which, by a strange visitation, became the home of the Demeter "mysteries." Thousands of Athenians came here in procession each year for the solemn ritual of initiation. It was a religion based on the dramatization of death and resurrection and was very properly placed in the Gospel that included the story of Nicodemus (John 3:1-21).

The annual ceremonies were laced with strong emotion and carefully designed to promote the idea that a death to an old life was experienced and that those who believed were "born again." Initiates were called to maintain a vow of secrecy, but it was known that part of the climax was a blaze of torches in a dark room and the uplifting of a sheaf of wheat, symbol of death and resurrection.

Only the basement of the temple is now visible, and there is little left of what must have been great splendor. On my only visit, over twenty years ago, the site seemed sadly neglected; but I remember, corroded by the fumes of the modern oil industry of the place, a door lintel carved with a sheaf of wheat.

Every Greek, including the visitors from the Decapolis, would know the origin of it all. In desperate search for her daughter Kore (The Maiden), Demeter the Earth Mother came in grief to Eleusis. Kore had been kidnapped by Pluto, ruler of the Underworld, to be his bride; and in sorrow and anger, Demeter sent sterility to the earth until her daughter should be found. The king of Eleusis kindly received the goddess, not knowing, like Abraham, that he entertained a divine being until strange events in the household made the goddess' presence felt. Demeter remained until Zeus forced a compromise, and Pluto surrendered his bride for six months of each year. Thus it was that winter and summer began their alternation. It is one of the many legends of resurrection that haunt all mythology—a sort of premonition of truth yet to be revealed. A "dream of the race come true," was how C.S. Lewis related such stories to the historic realities of the faith.

On her departure, Demeter gave as a present a grain of wheat to the little prince Triptolemos, eldest son of Celeus, her royal host. She told him to place it in the ground and expect a fruitful resurrection. So wheat came to bless the fields and tables of men. Because Demeter's Roman name was Ceres, we commemorate the myth with every "cereal" breakfast food we eat. The large relief in the Athens museum shows the small boy in the act of receiving the grain. Perhaps Christ saw in this legend, familiar to His foreign visitors, a truth that would be illustrated on Calvary and in the empty tomb.

The legend formed part of the oral and perhaps written tradition of early church, for in A.D. 57, or perhaps a year or two earlier, Paul had occasion to write to the turbulent little church on the Corinth isthmus. In his letter he revealed his knowledge of it (1 Cor. 15:35-38). Paul was intent on rebuking the dissident group in the congregation who were calling the historic fact of the resurrection into question. Perhaps at Corinth were converts from the Eleusinian mysteries who reminded Paul of the context. If he reached Corinth by road, his route could have passed Eleusis as he turned south out of Athens. Perhaps it was then that Paul thought of Christ and the transformation wrought in a grain of wheat. In Ephesus, as he wrote, the picture passed through his mind.

Pilate and the Trial

There is no trial in all ancient history better known in all its detail than the trial of Christ. And by a curious accident of history a minor governor, a procurator of Tiberius, occupied a central role. It is possible to tell from numismatical studies (and coins are prime archaeological material) and a few other scraps of evidence, how compelling circumstances forced Pilate into the role he was to play on that high and revealing stage.

The story is difficult to piece together because Pilate left no account of his own, nor did he find a friend to defend him. He was a stern and selfish man with few friends and many enemies, intractable, with an odd streak of cowardice. Pilate was the last man who should have been governor of Palestine.

When he sat on the judgment seat that morning at the place called the Pavement, Pilate was facing the fruits of folly. Pontius Pilate is mentioned by writers sacred and secular, Josephus, Philo, and the four Evangelists. On all occasions he won the right to reference by an act of obstinate folly. He had carried the legionary

"The Pavement."

standards into Jerusalem with the medallions attached; and so, by setting up an idolatrous portrait in the holy place, stirred the anger of the Jews.

The Jews, moreover, had beaten him on the issue. Josephus told the story of the standards.

Pilate, being sent by Tiberius as procurator to Judaea, introduced into Jerusalem by night and under cover the effigies of Caesar which are called standards. This proceeding, when day broke, aroused immense excitement among the Jews; those on the spot were in consternation, considering their laws to have been trampled under foot, as those laws permit no image to be erected in the city; while the indignation of the townspeople stirred the countryfolk who flocked together in crowds. Hastening after Pilate to Caesarea, the Jews implored him to remove the standards from Jerusalem and to uphold the laws of their ancestors. When Pilate refused, they fell prostrate around his house and for five whole days and nights remained motionless in that position.

53

On the ensuing day Pilate took his seat on his tribunal in the great stadium, and summoning the multitude with the apparent intention of answering them, gave the arranged signal to his armed soldiers to surround the Jews. Finding themselves in a ring of troops, three deep, the Jews were struck dumb at this unexpected sight. Pilate, after threatening to cut them down if they refused to admit Caesar's images, signaled to the soldiers to draw their swords. Thereupon the Jews, as by concerted action, flung themselves in a body on the ground, extended their necks, and exclaimed that they were ready to die rather than to transgress the Law. Overcome with astonishment at such religious zeal, Pilate gave orders for the immediate removal of the standards from Jerusalem.[1]

Catch the flavor in this story of a certain blend of arrogance and cowardice. Pilate was in a sense the victim of a divided loyalty. The decade in which he was prefect of Judaea was a tense one in Rome.(Note that prefect was the correct term at this time and is attached to Pilate in the first inscription to mention him—one discovered by Italian archaeologists in 1961.) He had one mandate from the unpopular but strong Tiberius, which was to keep the fragile eastern frontier at peace. However, Pilate, appointed in A.D. 26, was probably an appointment of Aelius Seianus, then immensely influential with the Emperor. At Seianus' secret suggestion, perhaps, he was treating the Jews harshly. Seianus might have had some purpose in sabotaging the peace of that frontier or else was on other grounds anti-Semitic. When Seianus fell in A.D. 31, discovered at last in his plotting against the emperor, Pilate was left in a delicate position. He had, however, compromised himself too much to draw back. In the incident at Caesarea we see his dilemma.

The withdrawal of the standards was an illuminating revelation to the Jews. They had summed up their governor and knew that his arrogance could be overridden by clamor. Observe that Flavius Josephus, the unlikeable Jewish secretary of the Emperor Vespasian has been extensively vindicated as a careful historian. That process continues as Professor Benjamin Mazar and his able colleagues continue their excavations of Jerusalem-outside-the-walls on the south and southeastern sides of the massive Temple Mount.

Later, should we choose to believe Philo in a matter passed over by Josephus, Pilate tried again, timidly or obstinately, to honor the emperor in Jerusalem, where he had not been honored before.[2] In Herod's palace he hung some gilded votive shields dedicated to Tiberius. The reaction was violent. Pilate faced immediately a deputation of the Sanhedrin and the four surviving sons of Herod the Great. The latter group, exploiting the influence their family had always enjoyed in Rome, appealed to Caesar when Pilate proved obdurate. Tiberius sent a curt order to his governor to move the shields to Caesarea to hang in the temple of Augustus. Pilate was shy of a further complaint because he had handed another advantage to his foes.

A third incident shows the same awkwardness, the same mingling of cruelty and timidity, and the same inability to cope with provincials. Josephus in the passage already quoted gives us another example of Pilate's methods.

> On a later occasion, he provoked a fresh uproar by expending upon the construction of an aqueduct the sacred treasure known as *corbonas*. The water was brought from a distance of 400 furlongs. Indignant at this proceeding, the populace formed a ring around the tribunal of Pilate, then on a visit to Jerusalem, and beseiged him with angry clamor. He, forseeing the tumult, had interspersed among the crowd a troop of his soldiers, armed, but disguised in civilian dress, with orders not to use their swords, but to beat any rioters with cudgels. From his tribunal he gave the agreed signal. Large numbers of the Jews perished, some from the blows which they received, others trodden to death by their companions in the ensuing flight. Cowed by the fate of the victims, the multitude was reduced to silence.

Pilate could clearly not afford another appeal to Caesar. It was dangerous to annoy further the old recluse of Capri. Add to the list of follies the sacrilegious massacre in Galilee mentioned in the Gospels (Lk. 13:1,2), and the sum of Pilate's mistakes assumes perilous proportions. This set the stage for the triumph of the priests at the trial of Christ. Their victory over the prefect, who was convinced of the evil of their accusations, came at a time when Pilate sought a way, within the limits of his cowardice and compromised career, to follow justice and release Jesus. Pilate sinned that day because his past was too powerful.

Coinage

Coinage is a major source of archaeological information. Coinage always meant something in the ancient world. Harold Mattingly, the late curator of Roman coins in the British Museum, showed how to trace whole tracts of policy and history in imperial times by the study of the contemporary coinage. People examined their coins for a message, and the coins were an instrument of policy. The Jews alone objected it was idolatrous to carry in their purses the image of a man. In typical Pharisaic fashion they compromised over the silver denarius, with its portraiture of Augustus or Tiberius, saying that it was really not theirs but Caesar's. That was the whole point of the Lord's devastating reply over the tribute money (Matt. 22:20-22).

Quite a different matter came when the land was deluged with common copper coinage that ran contrary to Jewish sentiment. Valerius Gratus, Pilate's predecessor, had tactfully issued coins harmlessly adorned with palm branches or stalks of wheat, familiar enough Jewish symbols, but as early as A.D. 29, Pilate issued copper coins bearing the *lituus*, or pagan priest's staff, a symbol of the imperial cult, which was bound to be obnoxious to the people. It was calculated provocation and comparatively safe, because the users were insulted individually; and the coinage did not produce collective demonstrations of hostility. Pilate also felt safe because with the tribute money the Jews were compromising over an idola-

Coins from the procuratorship of Pontius Pilate (A.D. 26-36).

trous symbol, the emperor's own portrait. Each man swallowed the new piece of arrogance and said nothing. Seianus fell in A.D. 31, and, significantly enough, the issue of such provocative coins ceased about this time.

Coins reveal something of the foolish and distracted man who sent Christ to the cross. Clearly, the Pilate of the offensive coins stung his enemies with the inscription over the cross and returned the savage answer: "What I have written, I have written" (John 19:22).

The coinage is, to paraphrase Professor Mazar from the massive edition of Josephus published by him and his colleagues, a witness to Pilate's inflexible personality, refuting modern attempts to rehabilitate him.

Caesarea

A brief footnote can be added to the story of Pilate. As recently as 1961 a slab of stone was discovered in Caesarea in the ruins of the Roman theater in the course of its quite magnificent restoration. The letters are fragmented.

...IBERIEVM
...IVSPILAT
D D D

Presumably, it means a Tiberieum, or shrine, for the worship of the Emperor Tiberius, "given, donated, dedicated" by Pontius Pilate. Here is the man again, so eager to be, as the Jews sneered, "the friend of Caesar." More might yet come of those extensive ruins on the open coast of Israel.

Caesarea lies on the open coast of Palestine. It is a rough and harborless shore where low sandhills are swept by the sea winds and the Mediterranean surf. The coast is strewn with ancient harbor works, where engineers have striven to provide a haven for ships. The sea has won in every case, and the endless assault of the waves has broken down and swallowed mole and breakwater all the way up the old Philistine coast to the jutting promontory of

Carmel, which provides Haifa with a modicum of shelter from the southwest winds.

At Caesarea the Mediterranean surge had its hardest task. Herod the Great spent twelve years, from 25 to 13 B.C., building

The Pilate inscription.

his great port there. The port was a matter of life and death for him to give the Romans a safe bridgehead. His subtle diplomacy aimed at serving Augustus, who kept him in power, and simultaneously at conciliating the Jews, his restless and resentful subjects. Hence the apparent contradiction of a temple to Augustus at Samaria and a temple to Jehovah in Jerusalem. This is a testimony to Herod's ruthless ability. He carried through this dual policy and, in the end, died in his bed.

Caesarea gave the Romans an entry and a base. The sea wall was a notable triumph of engineering. How the blocks of limestone, some of them fifty feet long, were put in place to form the mole, itself some two hundred feet wide and standing in twenty fathoms of water, is still not known. It would tax all the resources of a highly mechanized society. The sea wall curved around to form a haven. Behind it, on the low sandy shore, a semicircle of wall protected the town, its houses, racecourse, theater, and temples.

Nothing of Herod's harbor is visible from the boulder-strewn shore today, although the dry dock for the galleys may still be traced. The theater with its high curve of seats is prominent. There Pilate, for some reason, set up his inscription.

There are sundry Roman buildings on the crowded site. Somewhere among those stones Philip had his house, Cornelius his barracks, and Paul his cell. Crusader ruins dominate the scene, for the Frankish invaders saw the advantage of Caesarea as a beachhead, as clearly as did Herod and his Roman masters. North of the town is a vast aqueduct that brought in water from some distant spring and must have been the fortress' most vulnerable link. Surely somewhere the archaeologists must find vast storage tanks. Water would be a problem for the garrison even with uninterrupted command of the sea lanes. Pilate built an aqueduct into Jerusalem and built it with the forbidden temple funds. It would be interesting to know whether he gave such thought to the headquarters town.

Crucifixion

So Pilate "delivered Him to be crucified" (Matt. 27:26). Christ knew what He faced when He was on the road up from Jericho and as he knelt under the gnarled olives in the Garden of Gethsemane. For all the cluttering of that sacred site with the buildings of to-day's rival sects, there is the sense of a Presence there. Those in-credibly seamed and weathered trunks might be a millennium old; but the roots under the ground, spared Roman destruction in two revolts, are probably the roots that sought the moisture in the sparse soil and limestone crevices when the Lord faced His agony.

With His undimmed intelligence and acuteness of apprehen-sion, He could imagine the rending horror of it all, and on that theme archaeology has had a recent word to say. Fearful light on the crucifixion was shed by a discovery of 1968, in an ancient cem-etery at Giv'at Ha-Mivtar. In this Jerusalem cave, exposed by a bulldozer during road construction, Israeli archaeologists un-earthed some limestone chests, or ossuaries, the first material evi-dence of a crucifixion. It could indicate that Jesus Christ might have been crucified in a posture different from that shown on the traditional cross. A detailed anatomical study of the skeleton of a man crucified at about the same time as Christ (he was a young man named Yehohanan, that is, "John," Ha-Gaqol) showed that the victim was nailed to the cross in a sitting position, his legs slung sideways, with the nail penetrating the sides of his feet just below the heel.

The anatomical study of Yehohanan's tortured skeletal remains, carried out by Dr. Nico Haas of the Hebrew University anatomy department, indicated that the man was crucified "in a compulsive position, a difficult and unnatural posture," evidently to increase the agony. The feet were joined almost parallel, transfixed by the same nail at the heels, with the legs adjacent. The remains of the nail were embedded in the ankle bones. This single nail, which had fastened his feet to the upright post, had struck a knot that bent the point. This made it easier for those who took the body down to break the nail from the wood rather than to remove it from the feet.

The knees were doubled in a semiflexed position with the nailed heel bones showing the right heel overlapping the left. The torso was contorted and the arms stretched out, each apparently stabbed

Spike within the ankle bone of a crucified victim.

with a nail in the forearm, not in the palms. The arm bones were scratched around the nails by Yehohanan's agonised writhings, some two inches above the wrist bones.

Yehohanan's experience seems more historically accurate than the traditional art showing Christ with both palms nailed to the cross, His legs stretching straight downward, and a nail transfixing the feet frontally near the instep. Scholars in Jerusalem believe that the posture revealed in the anatomical report of Yehohanan indicated the usual position for crucifixion used at that time.

Although the Israeli scholars who discovered the remains say the man was crucified two thousand years ago, team member Dr. Avraham Biran, director of the Government Department of Antiquities, said it would be "mere fantasy" to think the skeleton might be that of Jesus Christ. The tomb at Gi'vat Ha-Mivtar was not empty, and the contention that the bones of Jesus lie somewhere in Palestine, remains as nebulous as the skepticism of the New Theology that advances it.

The Cross

Nor, for all the relic-lore of the Middle Ages, has any fragment of the cross survived. Roman nails, on the other hand, some of them in brand-new condition, were discovered in Scotland. These nails are a supply abandoned by Agricola when he withdrew from his reconnaissance into Scotland in A.D. 78. The nine-inch and six-inch spikes, sharp, heavy-headed, quadrilateral, in tough iron, are probably like the nails of the cross.

Philological and literary evidence seems to point to a cross in the shape of a capital *T*, and archaeology gives support to this premise. The upright stake was a fixture at the place of execution. The crosspiece was a beam carried by the condemned victim, bound to his arms and across the nape of the neck. This evidence was competently assembled by Dr. Barbet in his attempt to prove

A crucified victim upon a "T" cross.

the authenticity of the Turin Shroud, a major archaeological trea-sure.[3] Unfortunately, the actual history of the shroud cannot be traced back beyond the fourteenth century. But apart from this dif-ficult project Dr. Barbet's work has much of deep interest to say on the death of the Lord and His agony.

Archaeology might be expected to have some decisive word to say about the Crucifixion, but the evidence is not absolutely clear. A satirical third-century graffito from the Roman Palatine shows a line-drawing of a crucified ass, worshipped by a standing figure and labelled: "Alexamenos worships his God." The cross appears to be in the form of a capital T, but an upward protrusion behind the head of the animal could suggest the traditional form. A similar doubt arises in a representation of Christ on a third-century gen-stone. The cross appears in the form of a capital T, but a tiny chip on the gem above the head of Christ leaves a small doubt.

The early Christians shrank from all representation of the Pas-sion, and scarcely a score of crosses can be collected from the graf-fiti of the catacombs. The earliest crucifix ever discovered seems to have been made in the late fifth century and is of traditional shape. The same is the case with the oldest representation of the crucifix-ion, a rough miniature in a Syrian evangelarium, dated A.D. 586, now in the Laurentian Library in Florence. It must be remem-bered that by the date of these attempts to represent the Crucifix-ion, this form of execution had not been known since Constantine's abolition of the hideous practice between A.D. 315 and 330.

In one or two rare catacomb inscriptions, the cross in the form of a capital T seems to be inserted in the midst of a martyr's name. DionTysion, for example, in the Catacomb of Saint Peter and Marcellinus. M with a bar above it (the horizontal beam of the cross?) seems to be a similar indication of martyrdom inserted into an epitaph, e.g., VERICMVDVS (Vericundus). The T-device dates from the second and third centuries and might support the contention that this was the common shape of the cross.

NOTES

[1] Josephus, *B J* II 8.9.
[2] *Leg ad Gaium*, XXIII.
[3] Pierre Barbet. *The Passion of Our Lord Jesus Christ* , chap. 2.

6

ARCHAEOLOGY AND THE EMPTY
TOMB

There is no more important event in history than Christ's rising from the dead and leaving the tomb in the garden empty. Even Christ's bitterest Jewish foes, even the deeply concerned Romans, must have recognized the significance of the claim that Christ had risen from the dead. All hostile attempts to explain away the Resurrection have proved to be much more difficult to believe than the reports, simple and circumstantial, of those who spent their lives steadfastly maintaining they had seen the risen Lord.

But where was the new tomb in the garden and where was Golgotha ("Place of a Skull")? These should be the most important archaeological sites in Jerusalem. Since John's Gospel states that the tomb was in the immediate vicinity of Golgotha, there is in reality only one site and not two to be located. No word of ultimate certainty, however, can be said about the scene of Christ's death and burial. Christians are divided on the issue. Roman Catholics and the Eastern churches fervently favor the site in the great, crumbling Church of the Holy Sepulchre; others, principally Protestants, opt for "Gordon's Calvary" on the Nablus Road.

The Church of the Holy Sepulchre

So there are two claimants for recognition, and archaeology can provide no final guide. Deep in Arab Jerusalem stands the dark and shabby pile of the Church of the Holy Sepulchre. It contains more than a tomb. Along with a cave-like recess, lined and paved with marble slabs in a manner that forbids all archaeological investigation, is a bald outcrop of rock, which is, allegedly, the hill of Calvary. The present church, largely a Crusader building, is the successor to a large number of earlier edifices going back to Constantine, whose devout mother, Helena, chose the site. Even this church itself has been rebuilt many times right into the last century. Its custody is in Moslem hands. Its occupancy is divided between five ancient churches, whose liturgies and gyrations of worship can, at times of festival, come close to a lamentably embarrassing entanglement.

A rock-hewn tomb with rolling stone door.

Can this be the true site of Christ's death and resurrection? The question is complicated by rival loyalties and claims. Revolted by the confusion and the complete remoteness of the whole scene from anything the mind might envisage of that historic and awesome place, thousands have turned emotionally to the more satisfying claims of Gordon's Calvary on the road north from the Damascus Gate. But it should be granted that emotion can be a faulty guide to historical truth. It seemed initially absurd that this site in a northwest angle of ancient Jerusalem should be "outside the gate" (Heb. 13:12), until expert archaeological investigation carried out beneath so tangled and cluttered a site made a case for a first-century wall, which did actually exclude the hill of Calvary and the garden of Joseph.

The suggestion is that the hillock of Golgotha, before the scarping and vandalizing of which the early builders were quite capable, actually extended over a considerable area now overbuilt by centuries of reconstruction and remodeling. The stone outcrop inside the building is only a fragment and symbol of the original hill of Calvary and the tomb recess is in the same process, a mere shell remaining from an overbuilt garden. This could allow for a much greater distance between burial cave and place of crucifixion than what is presented within the old building of today. The ancient claimants of holy sites, in their tasteless endeavor to occupy and overbuild, had no care for preservation or for the sacredness of old contours and features of topography. The Garden of Gethsemane and the Bethlehem church are illustrations of this insensitivity. The desecration, for the same misguided reasons, of the synagogue of Capernaum and the mosaic floor of the Church of the Loaves and Fishes by Galilee within recent years are two more examples.

There arises another difficulty. Suppose archaeologists who assert the Herodian wall was where the outside location of the church required are correct in their deductions. Surely no defense engineer would leave just outside his elaborate fortification such a natural ballista platform as the undamaged Calvary would provide? Helena discovered it after two centuries of oblivion under the rubble of two Jerusalems, with all tradition surely broken by long neglect.

If some sensitive machine slung beneath a helicopter could reveal the layered remains of construction beneath the Church of the Holy Sepulchre and the ancient form of the unscarped hill and garden, we might be able to prove the authenticity of the site. In the present state of knowledge, claims that here lies the holiest place in Christendom cannot be accepted without reservations.

Gordon's Calvary

Unfortunately, the alternative site of Gordon's Calvary outside the Damascus Gate lacks equally final archaeological proof. Nonetheless, large claims to authenticity can be made. Amid the building of centuries and the distortions of ancient occupations, it is impossible in Jerusalem to recover a visual idea of the old geological patterns of hill and valley. Certainly, however, the garden tomb and the accompanying hill of death lay at the northern end of the same lift of land whose southern end is today occupied by the Temple area, and by the Moslem Dome of the Rock, the alleged place of Abraham's sacrifice.

The present Damascus Gate stands on the foundations of a Roman gate dated 20 B.C. The pattern of roads to this place is therefore an ancient one. The area of the lovely garden under the ridge is also free from superimposed building. The visitor can stand at ground level and consider that only human feet have smoothed the rock surface back to Crusader times. The only signs of building are the marks of a Crusader chapel, which are on the rock face of the low cliff where a tomb was cut, and on the level rock floor in front of it. The shrine appears to have backed on to the tomb door, evidently behind the altar.

Why was the site, then, lost for so long? Constantine's enormous authority was located where his church, first of the series, was erected in the fourth century. Moslems, and later a brutal Turkish regime, had no reason to respect Christian relics. Thus, a token alien tolerance for a monotheistic minority was met by the grudging recognition of the city edifice.

A Greek was the first to note the Nablus Road site in 1867. Strong credence was given to it in its dilapidated state by General

Golgotha (Gordon's Calvary).

Gordon of Khartoum in 1883. The present old-world garden is the work of a century's Christian care and reverence. Quite recently, in the days when Jordan held that portion of Jerusalem, the ugliest of bus terminals was built against the skull-like face of the cliff at its northern end. This action showed small regard for Christian sensibilities, if not a deliberate effort to obscure the uncannily close semblance to the decayed face of a skull.

The site of Gordon's Calvary possesses decided claims to authenticity. There is even some evidence that Hadrian sought to desecrate it after the second Jewish revolt in A.D. 135, by setting tokens of pagan worship in niches in the rock wall above and to the left of the tomb. It might seem strange that an emperor as powerful as Hadrian should not have made his desecration more spectacular than that apparent in the garden cliff, but not all the legions were equipped with engineering and seige materials. It was the Tenth

Legion that stormed Masada, and it is still not clear whether that powerful force of marine troops was still functioning in Palestine when Hadrian's army, badly mauled, laid the land in ruins. The demolition squads had all the Jewish places of worship, plus such Christian sites as the cave at Bethlehem, to deal with. If the garden tomb was revered, it was outside a devastated Jerusalem and might not have seemed important to completely destroy.

There is the fact that an anchor, a very early Christian sign based on Hebrews 6:19 and found in the catacombs of Rome, is cut into the rock. This artifact dates from about A.D. 200. The mass of other articles of archaeological interest, some of them from a well quite recently cleared, have not been competently recorded, dated, and published. Someone should undertake this task, so that the hosts of visitors, who find the garden tomb and its striking Calvary moving and convincing, should have their deep emotional acceptance supported by an overwhelming conviction of authenticity.

The Nazareth Decree

More than a half century ago one of the most notable archaeological discoveries of modern times threw light on the resurrection of Jesus Christ. The discovery was in the form of a simple slab of white marble from Nazareth, the hometown of Christ. The article was bequeathed by a German antiquarian named Froehner to the Louvre, where it was exhibited in the Cabinet des Medailles. Froehner acquired it, according to his catalog, simply as: "Slab of marble sent from Nazareth in 1878." He was an eccentric person but an archaeological collector of distinction. Froehner would be most unlikely to have been deceived or desire in the sphere of a cherished expertise to deceive others. If he so set down the origin of the Nazareth stone, the statement can be quite unreservedly accepted. On the other hand, as a collector, Froehner guarded his private treasures with jealousy. He derived a perverse and lamentable enjoyment from the mere possession of antiquities of which the world of scholarship knew nothing. And so, publication, to Froehner's mind, diminished his personal interest in possession and might attract thieves. When the strange man passed away, the great French museum became the owner of his collection. In 1930, a half century after its arrival in Europe, Michael Rostovtzeff, the notable historian, cast his eye on the rather irregular lines of clear Greek letters. He realized then the Louvre had possession of an epigraphical treasure of supreme importance.

> Ordinance of Caesar. It is my pleasure that graves and tombs remain undisturbed in perpetuity for those who have made them for the cult of their ancestors, or children, or members of their house. If, however, any man lay information that another has either demolished them, or has in any way extracted the buried, or has maliciously transferred them to other places in order to wrong them, or has displaced the sealing of other stones, against such a one I order that a trial be instituted, as in respect of the gods, so in regard to the cult of mortals. For it is much more obligatory to honor the buried. Let it be absolutely forbidden for anyone to disturb them. In the case of contravention I desire that the offender be sentenced to capital punishment on charge of violation of sepulture.

Need the significance be stressed of a decree concerning moving the stone coverings of tombs and extracting the bodies of the dead, which comes from the town where Christ lived? The scholars were not slow to move, and Cumont, a first-rate ancient historian, was quickly in the field with an account of the inscription, an attempt to date it, an analysis of the language, and an assessment of its significance.

After Cumont's article, which appeared in the *Journal of Hellenic Studies* in 1932, the field became a well-trodden one. Since then every Roman emperor, from Augustus to Hadrian, with the exception of Caligula, has been named as the author or promulgator of the Nazareth Decree. No overwhelming reason, however, has been put forward for abandoning a position originally taken by Italian historian Arnaldo Momigliano, who thought the decree a rescript of Claudius. If the edict came from the time of any emperor after Augustus, its Christian significance could hardly be less.

Rescripts

We have called the inscription on the Nazareth stone an edict or a decree, but such documents tended to be in better language than appears on the Nazareth stone. It reads like a somewhat heavy-handed translation of a Latin original. It probably came to Palestine in Latin and was translated into Greek for the perusal of the bilingual people of Nazareth by an official secretary. The inscription was probably a "rescript," a reply by the emperor to a specific request addressed to him by a provincial governor.

The tenth volume of Pliny's correspondence contains many replies of this sort from the pen of the Emperor Trajan, outlining in conversational rather than official style the prince's will on some matter in question. One of these rescripts is famous for the first outline of imperial policy in the matter of the rising Christian Church. Indeed, included also in this volume of quite invaluable letters and replies is a letter in which the governor of Bithynia actually made inquiry regarding the moving of the remains of the dead, which was followed by a reply containing the emperor's written judgment.

> Having been petitioned by some persons to grant them the liberty of removing the relics of their deceased relations on the grounds that their tombs were destroyed by age, or broken down by the invasion of flood waters, I thought proper, Sir, knowing that it is usual at Rome to consult the College of Pontiffs on such matters, to ask you, as head of that sacred order, what course you would have me follow.

Trajan replied briefly, and one imagines a little testily, for Pliny was a most assiduous correspondent.

> The obligation to petition the pontifical college is a hardship for the provincials, when they have just reasons for removing the ashes of their ancestors. It will be better, therefore, for you to follow the example of your predecessors, and grant or deny this liberty as you see reasonable.

This is a perfect example of a question and a rescript. If the Nazareth document is a rescript, it must have come to Palestine in reply to an official request for similar instructions regarding the opening of tombs. Curiously, the stone was set up at Nazareth and only at Nazareth, the town from which Christ came; He whose empty tomb had given the Christian church its gospel.

Why was the emperor, whichever emperor it was, stirred to such drastic threatenings? Capital punishment for the less heinous crimes was not a common feature of Roman law until the third century, when the lengthening shadows of social and legal decadence lay heavily across the Empire. What sort of question, or what flagrant abuse, moved a Roman ruler steeped in the legal tradition of his race to lay down such harsh provision in one part only of the empire, and that part the town of Jesus of Nazareth?

Date and Authorship

Two converging lines of evidence suggest that the inscription falls within the decade before A.D. 50. The style and execution of the lettering satisfy the practiced epigraphist that the work belongs to the first half of that century. This rules out three emperors, Augustus, Tiberius, and Caligula. The central Roman government did not take over the administration of Galilee until the death of its puppet king Agrippa in A.D. 44. No decree would have been set up in Nazareth by the governor of Syria or the procurator of Judaea before that date. The autonomy of the area might have been a legal fiction, but the Romans, of all imperialists, knew the value of legal fictions.

Consider, too, the incident at the trial of Christ. "But they were the more fierce, saying, He stirs up the people, teaching throughout all Judea, beginning from Galilee to this place. When Pilate heard of Galilee, he asked whether the Man were a Galilean. And as soon as he knew that He belonged to Herod's jurisdiction, he sent Him to Herod" (Luke 23:5-7). No Roman authority would presume to set up inscribed laws at Nazareth before A.D. 44. If the epigraphical conclusion that A.D. 50 is approaching near the latest date for work so styled and executed, then one could hazard a close guess about the emperor who sent the reply to Palestine.

It could have been none other than Claudius. Once we accept that statement, one or two points of confirmation immediately appear. Claudius was an odd person, a sort of Roman James I, who would have been much happier with his books than with officers of state. Ancient historians persisted in calling him mad; but the more Claudius' actual achievements are studied, the clearer becomes the impression that he was a man of learning and of no mean ability. He was probably a victim of some form of cerebral disturbance. His faulty coordination conveyed an unjust impression of subnormality. In his early years he was probably ridiculed and misunderstood to a degree that damaged his personality. As emperor, Claudius was anxious to carry on the religious reforms of Augustus. He was deeply informed about, and genuinely interested in, the religious situation in the Mediterranean world.

A long letter, for example, has survived in which Claudius sought to regulate the serious Jewish problem of Alexandria. This letter, certainly a rescript of great historical and constitutional importance, was found among the papyri in 1920. It appears to contain the first secular reference to Christian missionaries. It was written in A.D. 41 and expressly forbid the Alexandrian Jews "to bring or invite other Jews to come by sea from Syria. If they do not abstain from this conduct," Claudius threatened, "I shall proceed against them for fomenting a malady common to the world."

Note the language. It is the rather downright style of the Nazareth inscription, and the language of a man who had studied the Jewish religious problem and found it irritating. It would be surprising if Claudius, with these preoccupations, was not the first Roman outside the Middle East to hear of the Christians.

The *Acts of the Apostles* (18:2), confirmed by two Roman historians, Orosius and Suetonius, recorded that Claudius expelled the Jews from Rome. This was in A.D. 49, which coincides with the likely date for the Nazareth inscription. Suetonius added that Claudius acted thus because of rioting in the ghetto, "at the instigation of one Chrestos."[1]

The reference is obviously to Christ and, as Arnaldo Momigliano once insisted,[2] those who deny that Suetonius made the simple mistake of confusing two Greek words, *christos* (Christ) and *chrestos*, must undertake the difficult task of proving their contention. To suppose that the Roman biographer was referring to

Christ is undoubtedly more reasonable than any other suggestion.

The situation might, with much probability, be reconstructed. In the forties of the first century the first Christian preaching was heard in Rome, and the synagogue was in bitter opposition. Trouble in the Jewish quarter and a wave of arrests attracted the dual interest of the emperor. His curiosity over religion and his awareness of the Jewish problem was aroused, as well as to his predilection for dispensing Roman justice. He heard the case, which proved to be a strange story. The trouble, he gathered, was about one named Christ, who his followers believed "rose from the dead." The defense of the rabbis was obviously the Pharisaic version of the empty tomb as reported by Matthew (28:13). The high priests told the soldiers to say Jesus' disciples had the body.

There is a quite authentic touch of Claudius' well-documented whimsicality and carefulness in the result. Unable to decide the issue, he banished all Jews. He must then have made inquiries and heard from the authorities that the preaching of the gospel of the Resurrection was rife. "What shall I do?" asked the governor. Back came the rescript. "Quench the trouble at its place of origin by a stern decree." Or, if the inscription is not a rescript, it could be a quotation from one of Claudius' long letters on religious problems, dutifully set up by the local authorities.

If this reasoning is sound, three facts emerge. The first is that Christian preaching began in Rome much earlier than was once supposed and many years before the arrival of Paul. The second fact is that imperial action against the church must have begun with Claudius and not with Nero after the great fire in A.D. 64. Finally, it appears that in Rome, as in Jerusalem, the importance of the empty tomb was accepted even by the foes of Christ. And so, in a rescript of an emperor, the twentieth century reads the first secular comment on the Easter story, which is virtually legal testimony that Christ's tomb was indeed empty.

Emmaus

Some humble stones, which speak of the rising of Christ, lie seven miles west, down the hills that fall away from the northern road out of Jerusalem. Here stands the village of Amwas—Emmaus, of course. Two Christians, not apostles, were on the way home from the city late one spring afternoon. Perhaps the setting sun, sloping down behind the ridge towards the Mediterranean, blazed into their eyes. Could that be why they did not recognize the stranger who overtook and fell into step beside them, stirring their inner being with His words on Scripture and the fate of the Messiah?

If you go to Emmaus, and it should not be missed by pilgrims, do not go into the great church, the construction of which has obliterated reality. Go beyond it to the north where there is more than a hundred yards of cleared Roman road, recognizably so with its huge flagstone paving. On the north side is the ruin of what was once an olive oil processing plant; on the side nearer the church are the lower courses of some stone houses, one of them with a natural spring rising in the small front room. In one of them the risen Christ broke bread and was recognized when the two disciples saw His wounds as He raised the loaf in blessing.

The Nestorian Monument

And now, far beyond the bounds of the Roman Empire, to China for a strange archaeological footnote. It is a story worth telling in view of certain philosophies of modern Gnosticism, which seek to demythologize the central truths of the Christian faith. If Christ did not rise from the dead in strong historical truth, there is no Christian faith left. Once in old China a Christian church, cut off from Western fellowship, inadequately supplied with Scripture perhaps and eager for syncretism, tried to build a faith without a crucified and risen Christ. That church failed.

In Sianfu, in 1625, an inscribed stone was found that had lain buried for nine centuries. Workmen digging foundation trenches came upon a large monument, over seven feet high and three feet wide. It had been set up in A.D. 781 and contained a statement of Christian belief and a description of the arrival in A.D. 635 at Sianfu of a missionary from Tutsin, or Syria. The missionary's name was Olopan. There was also an account of the fortunes of the church he founded and a few other relevant details in verse and prose.

It was an artifact of early Christianity in China and undoubtedly genuine. Edward Gibbon, whose skeptical and penetrating mind left nothing unexamined, accepted the evidence without hesitation. In chapter 47 of his famous *Decline and Fall of the Roman Empire*, Gibbon described the scattering abroad by homeland persecution of the followers of the fifth-century Syrian bishop, Nestorius. They fled east to Socotra, Ceylon, India, and China. "In their progress by sea and land," wrote Gibbon, "the Nestorians entered China by the port of Canton and the northern residence of Sigan." This was Sianfu.

They found persecution again. Gibbon continued:

> The mandarins, who affect in public the reason of philosophers, are devoted in private to every form of popular superstition. They cherished and they confounded the gods of Palestine and of India; but the propagation of Christianity awakened the jealousy of the State, and after a short vicissitude of favor and oblivion, the foreign sect expired.

Then Gibbon added a footnote.

> The Christianity of China, between the seventh and tenth centuries, is invincibly proved by the consent of Chinese, Arabian, Syrian and Latin evidence. The inscription of Sianfu which describes the fortunes of the Nestorian Church is accused of forgery by La Croze, Voltaire and others, who become the dupes of their own cunning while they are afraid of a Jesuistical fraud.

The forgery charge survived until Renan, but the Nestorian monument is now accepted as a genuine document. But why did the matter suggest more modern heresies? It was simply the reflection that the attempt to recast basic Christian doctrine in the terminology of an ephemeral philosophy, the current vice among theologians, has led to the collapse of the church on earlier occasions. To recast was precisely what the Nestorian missionaries in China sought to do, and no exception can be taken to an effort to preach a vital message in language that the immediate audience will understand. This is beyond all dispute the way to preach persuasively.

But, and here is the rub, the content of the preaching must not, in the same act, be eroded, attenuated, or lost. One can search in vain through the mystical and highly philosophical language of the Nestorian inscription for a clear statement of the two central doctrines of the New Testament, the atoning death of Christ, and the Resurrection, which was its confirmation. The ethical content was there, and the return of the Savior to heaven, but the rest was gone.

Why? Over the century and a half since the coming of the first valiant missionaries, the Chinese church had won a measure of favor in high imperial circles, but the church had also been aware of the suspicion and dislike of the philosophically minded, educated classes. Rightly, the Christians went to great lengths to bridge the gap between the doctrines they had to teach and the thought and language of those whom they sought to influence. And, as so often happens in such contexts, they went too far. They lost the real content of their message, just as the rationalist theologians of today have done in their encounter with existentialism.

The result? The church died. It was dry rot, not persecution, suicide, or murder. The Japanese scholar, P.V. Saeki, who studied the Nestorian inscription intensively, believed that the Nestorian Church still exists in two forms. The twenty million Moslems of China contain a host of its descendants. Unfortunately, they have been left with only a vague monotheism; a union that is an ecumenism with a vengeance. Other Nestorian descendants are the secret society followers of the "religion of the pill of immortality," which seems to contain in creed and ritual some vestigial memories of Christianity.

NOTES

[1] *Claudius* 25:4.
[2] *Claudius the Emperor and His Achievement* [1962].

7

ARCHAEOLOGY AND THE FOURTH GOSPEL

Before passing to the story of the beginning of the church, a brief word is needed about John's Gospel, the last of the four to be written and yet stamped most clearly with the marks of the eyewitness. There are a few matters in that remarkable book that cannot be passed by in any treatment of New Testament archaeology. John's Gospel is a priceless document of the faith. Its authority can hardly stand if its authorship is questioned; or if its writing is relegated to another century than the first.

The Assault on John's Gospel

John's Gospel is in a more vulnerable position historically, a fact which hostile critics have readily recognized. William F. Albright, dean of Palestinian archaeologists, remarked that Rudolf Bultmann in particular has carried on against this book an unremitting campaign for decades.[1] Such critics claim that John's Gospel contains virtually no original historical matter, but instead reflects an "early second-century Christian group tinged more than a little by Gnosticism."

The project of late-dating John's Gospel has therefore been pursued with some vigor; for even if it were allowed that the Gospel was written twenty years later, this would open the door to attractive revisionist possibilities. If it could be proved that John's Gospel merely set forth what the writer thought Jesus might have said,

79

had he lived in the early decades of the second century, then our contemporary revisers of Christianity would have a precedent for rewriting the Gospels as often as the mood of the moment might suggest. Revisionists could then put into the lips of Christ whatever sheer romance, narrow prejudice, or special pleading might imagine.

In fact, there is no valid reason at all for discarding the ancient tradition that the book was written by John, the last of the apostles to die. John wrote his Gospel in extreme old age, perhaps in the first half of the last decade of the century. He wrote to refute certain errors that were creeping into the church, which made his whole apologetic approach an appeal to history. His last chapter is a striking illustration. He clearly intended to finish his book with the closing words of chapter 20, and then found himself confronted with a nascent legend about his own immortality. Wearily he took up his pen again and refuted this tale. He did so by telling plainly the story of the walk by the lake, which had previously been misreported and misused. A.T. Olmstead, the historian, quoted by W.F. Albright, maintained that the narratives of John represent the very oldest written tradition, antedating A.D. 40.[2]

But what of the evidence that has made it so difficult for liberal criticism to undermine the apostolic authority of the Fourth Gospel? Consider tradition, which has a proven, heavy weight in such matters. In his letter to Florinus, a gnostic Roman presbyter, Irenaeus, who became Bishop of Lyons in A.D. 177, claimed direct contact with the Apostle John through the aged Polycarp, Bishop of Smyrna. Irenaeus had been a pupil of Polycarp who was a pupil of the Apostle John. Irenaeus claimed in the letter that the orthodox bishops and not the Gnostics were the successors to the apostles and bore truthful witness to the apostlic tradition. In another work,[3] Irenaeus states that John the Apostle wrote the Fourth Gospel in his old age at Ephesus.

Some Relevant Archaeology

Arguments more concrete for the traditional authorship and date are remarkably varied. Many of these arguments arise from

Papyrus 28, showing John 6:8-12.

archaeology. For the last fifty years some tattered fragments of the
New Testament were kept in the John Rylands Library in Manchester. They include a broken fragment of John's Gospel, which
remained unnoticed from the date of its acquisition in 1920 until
1935, when C.H. Roberts recognized their unique importance.
The fragments bore two sections of chapter 18, verses 31 to 33,
and 37 and 38, and the handwriting could be dated in the reign of

Trajan or of his successor Hadrian. Trajan died in A.D. 117, Hadrian in A.D. 138. Pick a point in the middle of Hadrian's reign, say A.D. 126, when his British garrison was building that astonishing symbol of empire, the wall across northern Britain. At that time John's Gospel was already known and being copied in Egypt. Indeed, one copy had been worn out and discarded. On that tiny piece of brown papyrus much fantasy was wrecked, along with an

Excavations at Pool of Bethesda, Jerusalem.

old attempt to thrust the Fourth Gospel deep into the second century.

This is not the only piece of archaeological evidence placing John's Gospel inside the life span of John of Galilee. The story of the Bethesda pool in Jerusalem (John 5:1-9) provides another example. Alfred Loisy, the French liberal scholar, suggested that John, or whoever wrote under that name, had altered the traditional tale to include the five colonnades. This, said Louisy, was to represent the five books of the Law that Jesus had come to fulfill. In other words, John's reference to five colonnades had no historical basis, but was invented by him to prove a theological point. Recent excavations revealed that before A.D. 70 there existed a rectangular pool with a colonnade on each of the four sides, and a fifth across the middle. As late as the thirties of this century, Loisy was teaching that the earliest date possible for the Fourth Gospel was at least a decade later than the latest date suggested by the Rylands papyrus.

Loisy's mid century date for the Fourth Gospel was itself a retreat from a more radical position taken by such liberal critics as those of the Tuebingen School of the nineteenth century. The discovery of Tatian's *Diatesseron*, the popular harmony of the Gospels compiled by the Tatian around A.D. 170, was the rock on which this radical criticism was wrecked. A papyrus fragment from Dura Europos, discovered in 1933 by C.H. Kraeling, consists of fourteen fragmented lines. This document revealed that Tatian's harmony of the Gospels was the first written in Greek (Syriac and Greek were linguistic competitors), and that it contained John's Gospel in the earliest of its versions. The fragment is an account of the request for the body of Christ made by Joseph of Arimathea.

In recent years the discovery of gnostic documents from Chenoboskion (Nag Hammadi) in Egypt, mentioned in the pervious chapter, almost rounded off modern knowledge of the gnostic heresies castigated by the church fathers. It became obvious that the Gospel of John in no way reflected such thought, while there was a strong affinity with the language of the Qumran sect. John was using the spiritual vocabulary of an early Judaism, rather than a later Gnosticism.

Further Evidence

A few minor points of archaeological confirmation remain. In the catacombs the raising of Lazarus, a story confined to John, appears in early murals. One in the Capella Graeca of the Priscilla Catacomb must be early second century. The vine and the branches form a mural theme in the first-century house of Hermes; but the decoration is, of course, difficult to date. An epitaph composed for his own tomb by Abercius, the bishop of Hierapolis (not Hierapolis of Asia), who died in the middle of the second century, seems to refer to John 6:68 ("Lord, to whom shall we go?"), and to the shepherd parables of John 10. If Abercius was seventy-two when he died, he must have lived before John's Gospel was written, and he may have known the writer. His references to "the Shepherd" therefore had a more than usual significance. The epitaph was discovered by William Ramsay.

W.F. Albright devoted several packed pages to archaeological confirmation of topographical and geographical allusions in John, which were at one time rashly supposed to indicate that the author was not familiar with the territory; Albright identified all the sites.

The same is true of "the Pavement" of John 19:13. Jesus was brought before Pilate in a place called in Greek the *lithostroton*, literally "stone pavement", (*Gabbatha* in Aramaic, literally, "ridge," or "elevated platform"). It was assumed that this paving was at the praetorium, near Herod's palace and the Jaffa Gate. Pere L.H. Vincent discovered, however, a fine early Roman pavement under the *Ecce Homo* Arch that originally measured almost three thousand square yards. He established that this paved area was, in fact, the courtyard of the Antonia fortress on a rocky elevation standing out above the surrounding area and properly called by the Aramaic name. The *Ecce Homo* Arch was built over the Pavement after it had been covered by the ruins of the Antonia fortress by Roman builders during the reign of Hadrian. The discovery strikingly illustrates the accuracy of the topographical nomenclature of John. He was describing a pre-A.D. 70 situation.

The term *rabbi*, thought to be a second-century title, has also been identified on bone containers called ossuaries and obviously dated before the destruction of Jerusalem in A.D. 70. Ossuary inscriptions verify the names of all the principal characters in the book (including Lazarus as the Hellenized form of Eleazer). The "striking archaeological confirmation of the Greek and Aramaic names preserved in John," concluded Albright, "cannot be accidental."[4]

It is sometimes said that archaeology proves the Bible. This is not quite true. Conservative scholars would rather say that the new discoveries consistently confirm the truth and authenticity of the Bible narratives, authenticate the text, and often illustrate vividly the events. More than in most cases, the archaeological contribution to the study of the Fourth Gospel has proved that small book's worth and relevance to the Christian faith.

The tattered remnants of John's Gospel found among the papyri of Oxyrhynchus in Egypt should be held in reverence. They are remains of Scripture at one time in the hands of poor men and go back in many cases to the third century. They were inked by unknown hands on the papyrus sheets as close to John's own time as today is to the Declaration of Independence. Broken, half-illegible, but always true to the text of the great manuscript rolls and codices on which our accepted text depends, the marks on the torn fibers spell out the same familiar verses which make John's Gospel a spiritual treasure. The Gospels could not do without their fourth and final message from the hands of the aged John.

NOTES

[1] William Foxwell Albright. *The Archaeology of Palestine* [1949] p. 243.
[2] *Op. cit.*, p. 243.
[3] *Against Heresies*, iii. 1.1.
[4] *Op. cit.*, p. 245.

8

ARCHAEOLOGY AND THE BIRTH OF
THE CHURCH

The fifth book of the New Testament, the Acts of the Apostles, is a work of ancient history in its own right. This account is the writing of a first-class historian, Luke, the physician of Antioch of Syria and Philippi of Macedonia. How the historicity of Luke's first-century narrative was vindicated is a matter of deep interest.

We have already mentioned in discussing the beginnings of papyrology the name of William Ramsay, classicist, archaeologist, and historian. Ramsay, later knighted for his services to scholarship, initiated the wide researches in Asia Minor and especially in the old Roman province of Asia. His research did much to vindicate Luke's accuracy and reliability as a historian.

Ramsay was Professor of Humanity from 1886 to 1911 at Aberdeen. During the tenure of this chair he traveled extensively in Asia Minor. He established a reputation for historical geography with his magnificent work, *The Historical Geography of Asia Minor* (1890) and books on the church, the Roman Empire, and the journeys of Paul.

The remarkable fact about the whole story, so relevant to the archaeology of the New Testament and its continuing romance, is that Ramsay set out with no thought of championing a conservative approach to Luke's work. Beyond a respectable Victorian's conformity and a sound scholar's desire for truth, he had little religious conviction and no belief in the authority of the New Testament or its worth as an historical document.

Ramsay worked during the heyday of destructive criticism begun in the universities of Germany. The breakdown of German Christianity and the vast weakness of a still convalescent Christendom are two visible results of the reckless scholarship beginning with Julius Wellhausen, and others, which left no tradition unassailed.

Ramsay, the future champion of Luke and Paul, accepted with little question the popular contemporary verdict that the Acts of the Apostles was a late second-century piece of imaginative reconstruction. The young scholar had no intention of spending the three years available under his research grant in anything so trivial as the discredited records of the New Testament.

The compulsion of fact at work upon an honest mind brought about the change. Acts 14:6 states: "they...fled to Lystra and Derbe, cities of Lycaonia." In other words, in passing from Iconium to Lystra, one crossed the frontier. Most geographers, basing their contention on what appeared to be competent ancient authority, dismissed the Lucan statement as a mistake. Local inscriptions, obviously more trustworthy than ancient or modern geographers, convinced Ramsay that the writer of Acts was correct. The frontier of Lycaonia lay where he said it did.

Turn of the Wheel

Here, then, in a paragraph, is Ramsay's own testimony written in 1898.

I may fairly claim to have entered on this investigation without any prejudice in favour of the conclusion which I shall now attempt to justify to the reader. On the contrary, I began with a mind unfavourable to it, for the ingenuity and apparent completeness of the Tuebingen theory had at one time quite convinced me. It did not then lie in my line of life to investigate the subject minutely; but more recently I found myself often brought in contact with the book of Acts as an authority for the topography, antiquities and society of Asia Minor. It was gradually borne in upon me that in various details the narrative showed marvellous truth. In fact, beginning with the fixed idea that the work was essentially a second-century composition, and never relying on its evidence as trustworthy for first-century conditions, I gradually came to find it a useful ally in some obscure and difficult investigations.[1]

History traveled far from those disreputable days when Ferdinand Christian Baur (1792-1860), the founder of the lamentable Tuebingen School of New Testament criticism, could speak of affirmations from the Acts of the Apostles as "intentional deviations from historical truth."

In 1963, the Oxford classicist and historian A.N. Sherwin-White published his Sarum Lectures of the previous year under the title Roman Society and Roman Law in the New Testament. This historian wrote with all the distrust of unsupported evidence proper to his profession and was a trifle ironical over the skepticism and fanciful theorizing of New Testament form critics. Sherwin-White disagreed with their gloomy conclusion that "the historical Christ cannot be known, and the history of his mission cannot be written." Classical historians, he gently pointed out, pursued with considerable confidence the truth about Christ's "best known contemporary," Tiberius Caesar, second imperial ruler of Rome. It might be added that the chief source for this dour and able prince is the historian Tacitus, who wrote seventy years after his death and with bitter prejudice against his memory.

Sherwin-White reached Ramsay's conclusions. Speaking of Luke's history he underlined the exactitude of the historical framework, the precision of detail of time and place, and the feel and tone of provincial city life, as seen through the eyes of an alert Greek and first-generation Christian. Luke's book, he wrote, "takes us on a conducted tour of the Greek and Roman world with detail and narrative so interwoven as to be inseparable." He showed that not only could the story have not been written in the second century, but indeed could not have been so written except at the time it had always claimed.

The Cities of the Eastern Empire

Let us follow Paul considering the archaeological evidence only. One of Ramsay's major contributions to New Testament studies depends almost entirely upon archaeological or rather epigraphical evidence. The mute and solid evidence of one inscription set Ramsay on the course of establishing Luke's reputation as an historian. Evidence from the area of Paul's first missionary activities in central Asia Minor, in the area of Iconium, Lystra, and Derbe, led to the "south Galatian theory."

Phrygia was an ancient country of Asia Minor noted in legend and history. It was immensely rich, for it straddled the ancient trade routes, and its civilization was early and precocious. In Roman times the area was comprehended in the provinces of Asia and Galatia. Of the latter province the northern portion was wild and uncivilized, populated largely by descendants of the Gallo-Celtic tribesmen who had broken into Asia Minor in an old tribal migration, giving Galatia its name. The southern portion was civilized and sophisticated and included such great cities as Iconium and Antioch.

It was previously assumed that Paul's Galatian churches were in the north. The assumption was based on numerous vague notions—that southern Galatia was Greek not Phrygian, that the instability of the Galatian church was a fruit of Celtic headiness, and so forth. The careful collection of epigraphical evidence proved again that Luke's geographical terminology (for example in Acts 16:6) could not be, as Ramsay phrases it, "more precise, definite, and clear."

One inscription speaks of the "Phrygian" Antioch. Other inscriptions make it quite obvious that the administrative district of South Galatia was Phrygian in language and tradition. There was, moreover, an uprooted minority of Jews, whose presence accounts for the Judaistic tendencies in the church. It is clear, too on epigraphical as well as historical evidence, that the whole area saw one of the earliest triumphs of Christian evangelism. There is an enormous corpus of Christian inscriptions from the area. And considering that the Crusaders marched through Asia Minor to Palestine without leaving one written memorial, the literacy of the Asian Christians was also emphasized.

Ramsay's demonstration that Galatia in the *Acts of the Apostles* was South Galatia answered the contentions of those who regarded the book as an unreliable fabrication of late origin. The Galatian passages in Luke's book could only have been written by a first-century historian who spoke naturally in the geographical terminology of contemporary inscriptions.

Apart from abundant coinage and inscriptions, no remains survive from the first-century cities of the area. Lystra and Derbe have been located, but few traces remain. Iconium, the modern Turkish town of Konya, was as lively then as today. In Lystra, to which Paul escaped from Iconium, an inscription was found dedicating a statue to Zeus and Hermes. The two deities were evidently linked in a local cult. The two, latinized in the King James Version as Jupiter and Mercury (Acts 14:12-13), and joined in the local myth of Philemon and Baucis were the deities with which the enthusiastic Lycaonians tragically identified Paul and Barnabas. Ovid, who told the story of Philemon and Baucis, had latinized the names, and there is more than one piece of evidence that the King James translators, knowing Latin rather better than Greek, kept Jerome's Vulgate open at their elbow. So the priest was recorded as the priest of Jupiter-outside-the-gate (Acts 14:13), as one might say: "Saint Martin's-in-the-Fields." Not far away at a town called Claudiopolis, in honor of the emperor, there is archaeological evidence of a temple to Zeus-outside-the-gate.

We are following Paul chronologically and so, for convenience, shall leave Ephesus to be dealt with along with the other cities of Asia in the chapter on the Apocalypse. Paul then moved west to the province of Asia, which occupied a ragged square at the Aegean end of the Asia Minor peninsula. The point of departure was Troas, which should not be confused with Troy, which now remains in ruins on an escarpment several miles away.

Troas, the western port of Asia, Paul's departure point for Europe, and perhaps the place of his arrest sixteen or seventeen years later, was a prime place of romantic ruin-gazing centuries ago when it was thought to be the Troy of Homer and early Hellenic history. There are, however, no readily identifiable remains of first-century history, and nothing connected with Paul's significant activity there, although this might be a suitable place to mention a papyrus relevant to Paul's return visit on the way home from Philippi.

This papyrus concerns the story of the boy Eutychus, who, overcome by the fumes of the oil lamps and perhaps no less by Paul's monumental sermon (Acts 20:9), fell from a high window. No proof is needed that fallible mortals can fall asleep during the best of sermons, or that a fall from a high window ledge can have tragic results, but it is curiously interesting to find a second-century papyrus containing a report of a similar accident.

> Hierax, governor of the Oxyrhynchite nome, to Claudius Serenus, assistant. A copy of the application which has been presented to me by Leonidas is herewith sent to you, in order that you may take a public physician and inspect the dead body referred to and after delivering it over for burial make with him a report in writing. Signed by me. The twenty-third year of Marcus Aurelius Commodus Antoninus Caesar the lord, Hathur 7.
>
> To Hierax, governor, from Leonidas, having Tauris for mother, of Senepta. At a late hour of yesterday the sixth, while a festival was taking place at Senepta and castanet-dancers were giving the customary performance at the house of Plution my son-in-law...his slave Epaphroditus, aged about eight years, wishing to lean out from the house-top of the said house to see the castanet-dancers, fell to his death. I therefore present this application and request you, if it please you, to appoint one of your assistants to come to Senepta, in order that the body of Epaphroditus may receive the necessary burial. The twenty-third year of the Emperor Caesar Marcus Aurelius Commodus Antoninus Augustus Armeniacus Medicus Parthicus Sarmaticus Germanicus Maximus, Hathur 7. Presented by me, Leonidas.

The Cities of Greece

Philippi and Thessalonica were reached by the Egnatian Way, or Via Egnatia, whose original terminus was Thessalonica. Both towns were old, and Philippi was renowned as the ancient capital of the founder of Macedon's empire, four centuries before Paul's visit. It is also the scene of some remarkable and recent important archaeological discoveries, notably the rich tomb of Philip II, father of Alexander the Great. But these discoveries are more relevant to Greek classical history, not the New Testament. Not many remains in either town are to be certainly related to the first cen-

Ruins at Philippi.

tury, save that both Philippi and Thessalonica contain vivid illustration of Luke's accuracy in the use of special terminology.

When Paul crossed from Asia into Europe, his chronicler described Philippi as "the foremost city" of the district (Acts 16:12).
Even the nineteenth-century New Testament scholar F.J.A. Hort
marked this down as a mistake, factual though he would have admitted the city's past greatness to have been. They relied on the
fact that *meris*, in Greek, never appears to have been used for "region." The Egyptian papyri, however, revealed that Luke's Greek
was better than that of his scholarly editor. The word, it was obvious, was quite commonly used for "district" in the first century,
and especially in Macedonia.

But another difficulty remained. It has been demonstrated with some likelihood that Luke came from Philippi. Had enthusiasm for his hometown led the physician astray, for was not Amphipolis the local capital? Loyalty did play a part, and the amiable foible is a clear mark of Lucan authenticity. But there was no distortion of fact, as Ramsay concluded:

> Afterwards Philippi quite outstripped its rival; but it was at that time in such a position, that Amphipolis was ranked first by general consent, Philippi first by its own consent. These cases of rivalry between two or even three cities for the dignity and title of "First" are familiar to every student of the history of the Greek cities; and though no other evidence is known to show that Philippi had as yet begun to claim the title, yet this single passage is conclusive. The descriptive phrase is like a lightning flash in the darkness of local history, revealing in startling clearness the whole situation to those whose eyes are trained to catch the character of Greek city-history...[2]

It is odd to see the personality of Luke the Philippian, peep out.

In the Greek text of Acts 17:6, 8, Luke twice called the rulers of the city *politarchs*. Since the term was unknown elsewhere, Luke's critics dismissed the word as yet another mistake. Yet, even today this word can be read high and clear in an arch spanning a street of modern Salonika, and sixteen other examples occur. A similar story of vindication could be told of the Greek title *protos* ("chief man"), applied in Acts 28:7, to the governor of Malta.

Paul came to Athens, where the Golden Age of Greece had its intellectual and artistic capital. As in Paul's day, Athens still lives on the splendor of that great age and the archaeological remains that illustrate it.

Looking down from the precipitous height of the Acropolis the visitor is aware of the fragments of Athens' agora, where Paul argued with the talkative Athenians. Closer at hand stands the great, chunky outcrop of rock called the Hill of Ares (Mars to the Romans). It was there, almost without a doubt, that the court of the Hill of Ares (the Areopagus) met. It was not a trial but a test Paul faced. The court seemed to have had some jurisdiction over who could and who could not give public instruction in Athens. The city had a reputation as a university center to maintain.

The Aeropagus (Hill of Ares).

In a brilliant speech the apostle used the Athenian environment to illustrate what he had to say—the altars "to the unknown God" (Acts 17:23), for example. And then, when Paul spoke of God not being in man-made shrines, nor to be represented by the finest of human art (Acts 17:24,25), there above and before him were the glories of the Acropolis, the exquisite Parthenon, the temple of Erechtheus, and the two mighty statues of Athena herself, one in full view with glittering uplifted spear. It was a glorious sight, and Paul passed it by with a gesture—and the tolerant philosophers listened unmoved. So, in one brilliant page, the greatest center of ancient culture moved in and out of the story of the New Testament and the birth of the Christian church.

The City of the Isthmus

The road winds down from Athens and over the deep trench of the Corinth canal, a project dreamed of by Nero but abandoned during the emperor's stay in Greece. The proud praetorian guards, who were employed on the task, doubtless proved a difficult labor force. The road ascends as it moves south; and the apricot roofs of modern Corinth come into view, with the Corinthian Gulf running into the mauve distance to the west and the blue Saronic Gulf to the east. In late summer there is the heavy smell of drying currants in the air, and the visitor remembers that the word *currant* derives from Corinth. And Corinth, like all the other place names ending in *inth*, like the words *plinth* and *labyrinth*, are words from the unknown tongue spoken in the Aegean before the Greeks came.

Further south, under the great precipitous outcrop of the Acrocorinthus, lies all that is left of old Corinth, once the cosmopolitan crossroads of the middle Mediterranean. In the great days of Greek independence and intercity strife, Corinth had been a naval

Temple of Apollo, Corinth.

power to challenge Athens. When Roman imperialism spread eastwards and Achaea became a province, the port inevitably became a nodal point of communications and a busy center of trade. The dragway by which the ships were hauled over the isthmus is still traceable.

Corinth was at strife with Rome in 146 B.C. and was destroyed in one of the most ruthless acts of vandalism in Roman history. Of the Corinth that fell, only seven Doric columns of the temple of Apollo, spared by the superstitious demolition squads, remain standing, high and prominent above the market place of the later town. When Paul reminded the Corinthians that the body was "the temple of the Holy Spirit" (1 Cor. 6:19), it would inevitably be this ruin that would rise to the mind's eye, windswept, clean, prominent for all to see.

Almost exactly a century after Corinth was beaten to the ground, Julius Caesar restored it under a wide colonization scheme thwarted by the senseless act of his assassination. It was Caesar's Corinth that Paul visited almost a century later still, and where, in the midst of the polyglot and cosmopolitan population of a notoriously vicious port, he founded the most troublesome and difficult of his Christian communities. It is also Caesar's Corinth on which the archaeologists have worked so busily, uncovering the agora, or market place, and part of the roads running down to Lechaeum, the port on the Corinthian Gulf, and Cenchrea, the twin landing place on the Aegean side of the isthmus. On the Lechaeum road a fragmentary inscription marks the synagogue of the Jews where Paul preached. Across one end of the excavated market place runs a stone platform, six to seven feet high, faced with marble. It is the bema where Gallio, Seneca's brother, sat to hear the case of Paul. His governorship, incidentally, is dated A.D. 52 by an inscription at Delphi. A tantalizing block of marble found near the theater bears another fragmentary inscription. "Erastus, for the office of aedile, laid this pavement at his own expense." Is this Erastus, the city treasurer, who was a foundation member of the Corinthian church (Rom. 16:23)?

Curiously, in the two major cities of Greece the story of Paul's ministry in Luke's book is linked with two temples. Paul never forgot the sight of Apollo's temple on the ridge when he saw it against the northwestern sky as he turned from Gallio's seat of judgment. This is obvious because the image of the temple appears in the two letters to Corinth three times.

NOTES

[1] W.M. Ramsay. *St. Paul the Treaveller and Roman Citizen* [London, 1898] pp. 7,8.
[2] *Op. cit.*, pp. 206,207.

9

THE ARCHAEOLOGY OF THE PERSECUTIONS

Christian epitaphs from the catacombs and other Christian graves have something to say about Rome's attempt to suppress the Christian faith. The sporadic persecution, which blotted two and a half centuries of imperial history, was Rome's most monumental mistake, contributing immensely to the weakening of the great world system Paul had hoped to infiltrate for Christ. The Roman Empire's choice of Caesar-worship as a bond of state was behind the policy of a few of the emperors, between Nero and Diocletian, who forceably resisted Christianity; but there were other roots as old and deep.

The Roman historian Tacitus wrote of Nero's use of the Christians as scapegoats for the great fire of Rome in the summer of A.D. 64. He recorded how the enormous cruelty of the mob was made possible by the unpopularity and gross misunderstanding of the church that Nero promoted. Evil dislikes confrontation with good, and a shockingly corrupt society dislikes the presence of a moral minority in its midst. Peter's first letter shows a deep preoccupation with the need for exemplary social conduct on the part of Christians as a visible refutation of pagan calumny. A graffito from the ruins of the Palatine hill in Rome reveals the ridicule Christians bore from baser members of society. The graffito shows a small figure, just possibly a soldier, with left hand raised in worship before a crucified figure with a donkey's head. The caption scratched upon it reads: "Alexamenos worships his god." Perhaps

Roman grafitto, *ridiculing Christians.*

it satirized a member of the city garrison or a student of the school for civil servants in operation near the forum. A few obscure epitaphs might suggest that there were Christians among the students. Was this "Caesar's household," which Paul mentions in writing to the Philippians (Phil. 4:22)?

Vested interests also had occasion to hate the Christians. In Pliny's letter to his emperor he stated that as repressive measures began to bite deeply, the sales of sacrificial meat (the meat mentioned by Paul in 1 Cor. 8:10) began to improve. In Ephesus those who earned their living from the corrupt worship of Diana raised a mighty demonstration (Acts 19:21-41). The great theater at the top of the axial road so characteristic of Greek cities still stands as a memorial to the chanting crowd. Indeed it has been massively restored. The officials of Asia or Asiarchs, who rescued Paul and whose office has been verified by archaeology, did not love Artemis (or Diana, as the Romans called her). They were the custodians of the imperial cult in the province of Asia.

However, perhaps by Nero's direction to justify retrospectively an act of bestial cruelty, or some time later, the proscription of Christianity found its way into formal law. This was dangerous, for a spiteful authority or a determined pressure group could always invoke the law, which made it difficult for a responsible offi-

The goddess Artemis (Diana).

Emperor Nero (A.D. 54-68).

cer not to act. During the period of perhaps five years in which Domitian oppressed the Church, it is fairly clear that the governor of Asia did his best to deflect harsh treatment from what he must have known was a stable element among his provincials. There is no archaeological or other evidence that Patmos was a prison camp, and John may have been at liberty to keep in communication with his provincials. Too, Domitian was confronted with evidence that Christianity had infiltrated his own family. Hence the name of Domitilla and her catacomb. He was simultaneously ravaging the senators and some Christians, who may have been associated with plots against him. Hence Peter's exhortation to Christians to mind their own business back in Nero's day. There was never a time in the first century when it was more likely to find a few upper-class Christians associated with plotting against a harsh tyrant, which Domitian was proving to be.

Two precious documents are found in the letters of Pliny, who governed Bithynia in A.D. 110-112. The province seems to have been almost Christianized, and it is a fair guess that the temple custodians and the butchers' guild were pressing an otherwise tolerant governor to apply the law. Pliny explained his dilemma to Trajan:

> In the meanwhile, the method I have observed towards those who have been denounced to me as Christians is this: I interrogated them whether they were Christians; if they confessed it I repeated the question twice again, adding the threat of capital punishment; if they still persevered, I ordered them to be executed. For whatever the nature of their creed might be, I could at least feel no doubt that contumacy and inflexible obstinacy deserved chastisement. There were others also possessed with the same infatuation, but being citizens of Rome, I directed them to be carried thither.
>
> These accusations spread (as is usually the case) from the mere fact of the matter being investigated, and several forms of the mischief came to light. A placard was put up, without any signature, accusing a large number of persons by name. Those who denied they were, or had ever been, Christians, who repeated after me an invocation to the gods, and offered adoration, with wine and frankincense, to your image, which I had ordered to be brought for that purpose, together
>
> with those of the gods, and who finally cursed Christ—none of which acts, it is said, those who are really Christians can be forced into performing—these I thought it proper to discharge. Others who were named by that informer at first confessed themselves Christians, and then denied it; true, they had been of that persuasion but they had quitted it, some three years, others many years, and a few as much as twenty-five years ago. They all worshipped your statue and the images of the gods, and cursed Christ.

Trajan, a stickler for law, replied that regulations were there to be enforced, but hinted that Pliny need not go out of his way to do so or heed anonymous depositions. Pliny, in a second letter, reported "the contagious superstition" was being contained.

> It is certain at least that the temples, which had been almost deserted, begin now to be frequented; and the sacred festivals, after a long intermission, are again revived; while there is a general demand for sacrificial meat, which for some time past had met with but few pur-

chasers. From hence it is easy to imagine that multitudes may be reclaimed from this error, if a door be left open to repentance.

It was obviously all distasteful to him, for his agents had infiltrated the Christians' meetings and found no truth in the allegations of disloyalty or cannibalism viciously alleged against them.

So it was everywhere over the first two and a half centuries. There were times when the fires flared up, as in Lyons in the time of the most philosophical of emperors, Marcus Aurelius. Under Decius, who had a legal mind like the great Trajan, there was an extensive attempt to apply the law. Whether it had been codified by the jurist Ulpian in his Digest not long before, we do not know; but Decius, in the interests of Roman unity set out to enforce Caesar-worship. This involved suppression of Christianity, and a form of declaration was drawn up of which several survive among the papyri. They illustrate Pliny's claim of the lessening numbers of Christians, as the unconvinced or the weak submitted to authority. Decius, fortunately for the suffering church, was in power only between A.D. 247 and 251. Perhaps persecution sifts the ungodly out, but how are the comfortable and unharrassed to judge the hard-pressed and the fearful? However, the papyri about apostasism could rather be certificates of loyal paganism and not necessarily renunciations of faith.

One such papyrus document was published in 1940, by Grenfell and Hunt, and was dated June 12 and July 14, A.D. 250. This was the time of Decius, when tidy-minded totalitarian bureaucracy was determined to sweep away the determined, dissident minority, which would not worship Caesar. The ritual of Caesar-worship was hardly more than saluting the flag and had the simple formality of a pinch of incense before Caesar's bust been accepted, the Christians would have been free to carry on unhindered the practice of their faith. They simply would not commit idolatry. The text of two of these *libelli*, as they were called, testifies that the Aurelian family were proper supplicants.

> To the superintendents of offerings and sacrifices at the city. From Aurelius...son of Theodorius and Pantonymis of the said city. It has ever been my custom to make sacrifices and pour libations to the

gods and now also I have in your presence in accordance with the commandment poured libations, made sacrifice and tasted the offerings, together with my son Aurelius Dioscuros and my daughter Aurelia Lais. I therefore request you to certify my statement.

A second document is similar.

To those chosen to have charge of the sacrifices, from Aurelia, wife of Ammonarios, from the village Theadelphia, and who always sacrifices and reverences the gods, together with the children of the Aurelian family, Didymos and Nouphios and Taat. We have ever continued to sacrifice and to reverence the gods with the children of the Aurelians, Didymos and Nouphios, and now in your presence according to the orders we have poured libations and have sacrificed and have tasted of the sacrifices, and I demand of you that you witness this with your signature for me. Farewell.

Both documents bore three signatures of witnesses to the pagan act. Possibly, the Aurelian family were Roman citizens who were taking some official post under Decius and were by regulation compelled to file a guarantee. If so, it signifies that the Christians had infiltrated secular society very deeply.

This theory might find support in a *libellus* filed by a priestess of the crocodile god, Petesouchos, and published in 1907. It was in the prescribed form and issued for "Aurelia Ammonous Mystos, priestess of Petesouchos, the great god." Either matters were such that Decius was requiring a reaffirmation of loyalty from those in religious office, or another member of the Aurelian family was once a convert to Christianity and was required to affirm her return to pagan allegiance. Or perhaps the Aurelians were falsely accused of being Christians. So, at any rate, in that day of judgment, the tares were sifted from the wheat.

There were those who did not sign renunciations of their faith. The day of trial tests and sifts. There are hundreds of known graves of those who gave their lives for their faith in Decius' day and in the two or three years of savage repression under a frustrated Diocletian from A.D. 303 to 305. Here was another able man who saw in uniformity and regulation the path to peace. One of the most recently completed excavations in the Lycus valley is the town of Aphrodisias, high up the river plain where stood Colossae, Laodicea, and Hierapolis. A full copy of the decree of Diocletian freezing wages and prices of the year 300 was found there. Diocletian lost that battle against inflation, but in its meticulous regulation and fierce sanctions the mind of the man is revealed.

10

THE PAPYRI AND THE EPISTLES

What J.B. Lightfoot called for in 1863, "letters written by ordinary people to each other with no thought of publication," was abundantly supplied by the epistolary material in the papyri. We must therefore look at the importance of the papyri's contribution to learning.

Letters were, of course, known well enough in Old Testament times, even among ordinary people. A famous archaeological find of half a century ago was that of the Lachish letters discovered by James Leslie Starkey in the ruins of Lachish, one of the outposts covering the approaches to Jerusalem and overrun by Nebuchadrezzar. These letters were scrawled in carbon on broken pieces of pottery and recorded an argument between the captain of the Lachish garrison and a junior officer, apparently over the controversial ministry of Jeremiah.

Thus it was that letters became the material of history. In the middle of the century before Christ, the great Roman orator and statesman, Cicero, wrote hundreds of letters, especially to his friend, Atticus. As the Roman Republic broke down in political turmoil and moved on to the dictatorship and murder of Julius Caesar and the beginnings of the autocracy we call the Roman Empire, it is possible sometimes to follow swiftly moving events week by week. Cicero intended sometime to publish his correspondence, but his own assassination left them unedited to pass on to posterity.

A century and a half later, the Roman aristocrat and senator, Pliny (ca A.D. 115), as governor of Bithynia, wrote nine books of

Lachish letter 4.

letters primarily for publication. His tenth book, containing information about the church, was Pliny's correspondence with the Emperor Trajan, and is a priceless letter file. The groomed and edited letters give historians insights into Roman life among the exalted. The line of important correspondence, edited and published, runs on to Jerome and Augustine (fourth century A.D.).

The poet Horace (ca. 30 B.C.) wrote letters in verse form, the subject matter sometimes contrived and sometimes a genuine communication whimsically classed as poetry. This mode of writing became a distinct form of literature; indeed it is a distinctive contribution of Rome to the literature of the world at large.

The letters of the New Testament are mainly didactic. They contain a large amount of personal detail and so are in the mainstream of ancient letter writing, but in general they were addressed to congregations of Christians. They were collected, probably at Ephesus, towards the end of the century, as the New Testament canon took shape. Two of John's letters and one of Paul's are highly personal. Paul's letter to Philemon, in fact, is remarkably like a letter Pliny wrote to a friend containing a similar plea for clemency.

The Papyrus Letters

The surprise of the papyri has been the vast extent of ancient literacy and the volume of the everyday correspondence between private persons on all manner of subjects. The nonliterary correspondence reveal the common man lost so often to view in literature at large. In these papyri historians were taken (as the Gospels sometimes take us) into the byways of life, the small back streets, the shops, and cottages. Hence the enormous historical value of these poor documents of life, apart from significant contributions they make to our knowledge of Greek in the days when the New Testament was written.

The subject matter is as wide as common life with all its pathos, sorrow, happiness, and joy. The papyri contain those small things that seem so important in the pattern of the days. For the first of some examples, one ancient papyrus letter, published in 1903, was written by a man named Serenos. The letter was addressed to his "sister" (that is, his wife), Isidora.

> Many greetings. Before all else I pray for your health, and every day and evening I perform the act of veneration on your behalf. I assure you that ever since you left me, I have been in mourning, weeping by night and lamenting by day.

The letter was not Christian, and the occasion cannot be guessed, nor indeed the nature of the act of worship mentioned. Sickness and health are often mentioned along with the common trials of life. The following example, a Christian letter, is probably from the fourth century, when Christian writing naturally became more prolific. It is only a fragment:

> ...to our God and gracious Saviour...I am writing this to you in sickness, very ill, and quite unable to rise from my bed...

Egypt was an unhealthy land. Bilharzia was a common peril as the peasants waded in the stagnant flood waters. Horrible infestations of enormous worms, arthritis, and the dental cavities promoted by the sand-ridden air were revealed by recent pathological investigations of common mummies. People suffered as they would suffer now over the physical trials of life. They were anxious, stressed, burdened. As poet A.E. Housman said: "the heart of man is never quiet, then 'twas the Roman, now 'tis I."

A Christian servant, again of the fourth century, wrote to his master concerning the illness of his mistress. "Please pardon me, my lord, and receive me kindly, though unwillingly I caused you such anxiety by the letters I had to write to you." Another mother and father of the century before wrote to their son to announce their recovery from ill-health and added a curious phrase: "up to the present time we have not sacrificed the pigs." Did they mean that their abandonment of pagan sacrifice still stood?

Some Schoolboys

One or two schoolboy letters appear in the collections. A fourth-century gem is found among the later Greek papyri listed in the index of the Loeb Classical Library Selections as: "Theon (spoilt boy), letter of, p297." His father seems to have slipped off to Alexandria with a weak half-promise to take the urchin with him unkept. Signing himself "Theonas," no doubt his pet name, he wrote:

> Theon to Theon his father greeting. You did a fine thing not taking me with you to town. If you won't take me with you to Alexandria, I won't write you a letter, or speak to you, or wish you good-day. And if you go to Alexandria I won't hold your hand, nor speak to you ever again. If you won't take me that's what's up! Mother said to Archelaus, "He upsets me, take him away!" It was nice of you to send me presents, big ones, beans, on the 12th, the day you sailed. Send me a lyre, please do. If you don't, I won't eat, and I won't drink. There now! I pray for your health.

In another letter the poor little lad Thonis was at boarding school, feeling the sting of his neglect, which a tactless teacher did nothing to allay. Observe the sad and homesick reference at the end about the lad's pet pigeons.

> To my lord and father Arion, from Thonis, greeting. I pray for you every day. Look, this is my fifth letter to you, and you have written to

me only once, nor have you come to see me. You promised me saying, "I am coming," but you have not come to find out whether my teacher is looking after me or not. And he himself asks everyday saying, "Isn't he coming yet?" And I just say, "Yes." Try then to come quickly, that he may teach me as he really wants to do. And when you come, remember what I have often written to you about. Good-bye my lord and father, and may you prosper many years along with my brothers, whom may the evil eye harm not. Remember my pigeons. To Arion from Thonis.

In another family the father, not the son, worried about the fees. It is easy to imagine what sort of a letter from home young Aurelius was answering, when he addressed his "very sweetest father." "I pray for you," he continued, "every day to the local deities. Do not be worried, father, about my studies. I am working hard and taking relaxation. It will be all right with me. I greet my mother." The letter then proceeded for a dozen lines with enthusiastic greetings to friends and relatives, a safer subject. Aurelius senior would doubtless have preferred some assurance about the relaxation.

There were other parents prepared to cut their worries at the root. A famous papyrus letter, dated actually from 1 B.C., is a comment on the grim, hard world to which Christ came with a charter for children. Hilarion, in search of work in Alexandria, wrote to his wife Alis at Oxyrhynchus. He addressed her as "sister," a term of endearment, although cognate marriage between brother and sister was permissible in Egypt.

Hilarion to his sister Alis very many greetings, likewise to my lady Berous and Apollonarion. Know that we are still in Alexandria. Do not be anxious; if they really go home, I will remain in Alexandria. I beg and entreat you, take care of the little one, and as soon as we receive our pay I will send it up to you. If by chance you bear a child, if it is a boy, let it be, if it is a girl, cast it out. You have said to Aphrodisias "Do not forget me." How can I forget you? I beg you then not to be anxious. The 29th year of Caesar, Pauni 23. Deliver to Alis from Hilarion.

There is something peculiarly horrible about the casual directions for the exposure and murder of a babe in the context of an affectionate letter.

Touching the problems of life, a note from a Christian priest to a Fayum cavalry commander is similar in purpose to Philemon 15 to 18.

> Greeting. I salute your children warmly. I would have you know, sir, concerning Paul the soldier who is absent from his unit. Pardon him this once...If he does not reform he will fall into your hands again in due course. Farewell, I pray, my lord brother, for many years.

The date is A.D. 346 and comes from a package of some sixty papyri in the office of Flavius Abinnaeus.

Epistolary Formalities

Example letters from papyri can illustrate all walks of life. From boys at school we could pass to soldiers on campaign, from husbands away from home to officials on circuit. Letters from the time when Luke was writing the Acts tell of the pickling of olives, a trip up the Nile, and the finishing of a new house. Children are mentioned. Reproaches to bad correspondents were penned. Rising prices were railed against. The delivery of a strong file that could deal with iron was requested. The style and the variety of content varies little over the four centuries covered by the Greek papyri.

When the New Testament epistles are compared, one notices that Paul observed with some care the forms of polite address common in his day. There was an opening word of salutation, followed by thanksgiving and prayer for the persons or company addressed. Then came the special theme of communication, greetings to friends, and perhaps a closing word of prayer. This second-century letter, for all its brevity, demonstrates the Pauline style.

> Ammonous to her sweetest father, greeting. When I received your letter and recognized that by the will of the gods you were in good health, I was very glad. And as at the same time an opportunity here presented itself, I am writing you this letter being anxious to pay my respects. Attend as quickly as possible to the matters that are pressing. Whatever the little one asks shall be done. If the bearer of this letter hands over a small basket to you, it is I who sent it. All your friends greet you by name. Celer greets you and all who are with him. I pray for your health.

The Scribes

One other point of some importance emerges from a study of the papyrus letters and that is the presence and function of the scribe. The body of the letter and the signature are seldom in the same hand. Letters were dictated, and even men and women capable of adding a signature and postscript in their own hand appear to have employed a professional letter-writer for the body of their note. In the epistle to the Galatians, Paul, in closing, took the pen from the scribe, and in "large letters" (Gal. 6:11) paid the church, which he had so sternly reprimanded, the compliment of a personal post-script above the signature that authenticated the whole. Or per-haps he was making a whimsical comment on the scribe's neat, small script and his own bolder hand. He, of course, used his col-leagues as scribes.

A capable scribe, aware of the mind of the writer of the letter, might have been entrusted, like any capable secretary today, with supplying some supplementary information or even expanding the text. Slight differences of style (as for example between the first and second letters of Peter) might easily be accounted for by the scribe's own phraseology in filling out a sketchy direction. One im-portant lesson, therefore, of the letters from the papyri, is the limi-tations of stylistic criticism, especially of the modern computer-generated variety.

Language of the New Testament

In the sphere of language the papyri have given much light to the student of the New Testament epistles and to the book as a whole. The nonliterary papyri revealed that Paul and his fellow-writers used the vernacular of the day and the racy speech of com-mon communication. What else could be expected? The politician, the demagogue, and agitator always realized the need to speak to people in the terms and patterns of their familiar intercourse. The aim of the New Testament writers was to be taken seriously, and its writers in consequence deliberately used the speech of ordinary folk in their daily routine. Luke began his Gospel with a piece of elaborate Greek worthy of Thucydides. Then as though in demonstrable and deliberate renunciation of all literary artifice, he rounded off his sentence and adopted the vernacular.

The same vernacular, recovered from the papyri, is the speech of the New Testament letters, and indeed, of the Gospels. It is not without grace and power; it is not incapable of poetry, as more than one chapter of Paul demonstrates. At the same time, it is in the full stream of contemporary Greek. And it is the vocabulary of that contemporary language which has thrown light on passages in the epistles obscure to the scholars who, before the coming of papyrology, approached the text only from the angle of classical and literary Greek.

Here are a few illustrations from the sizeable list of new words and new meanings, indeed, a growing list, which the papyri added to the Greek lexicon. "I have all, and abound," runs Paul's word to the Philippians in KJV (4:18). The meaning was obvious to the translators, but they had no means of illustrating this compound of the verb "to have" from any other Greek known to them, any more than they could do so in the three other New Testament contexts (Matt. 6:2, 5, 16). In translating the Lord's Aramaic: "they have their reward," Matthew used the same word as Paul did in the Philippian letter. Deissmann, the pioneer papyrologist, was the first to recognize from scores of receipted bills among the papyri, that in nonclassical commercial language this verb had assumed a new meaning, "to receive and give a receipt for," which is now the first meaning listed in the standard lexicon to the New Testament (Arndt and Ginrich).

An odd thought had crossed the mind of Matthew the tax collector. He pictured himself again at the customs office, writing scores of times a day the word that meant "he is quit," or "he has paid in full." He pictured the exhibitionist of the religious market place, "paid in full" in the sort of reward he valued. Paul was therefore saying: "You have paid me in full and something more." The recovered metaphor makes the verse more vivid.

Hebrews 11:1 recovered a metaphor also when a papyrus document revealed the word so vaguely translated "substance" was a word for "title-deeds." Title-deeds give secure possession of property that is not necessarily seen, and thus faith firmly places in our hands the unseen wealth of a spiritual world. For the same world Paul counted all worldly advantage "loss" (Phil. 3:8). His expression gained strength when it was discovered that a papyrus uses the same word for bones cast out for the dogs.

When the Jews of Thessalonica complained "these who have turned the world upside down" had arrived to disturb their peace too (Acts 17:6), they used a word Paul himself employed of those who were unsettling the folk of Galatia (Gal. 5:12) by pressing Judaism on the church. This was the very word Theon the schoolboy quoted in the letter mentioned earlier in this chapter. "He upsets me," the distracted mother complained.

In Romans 8:23, a Greek word is translated in KJV in accordance with its classical meaning of "firstfruits." It was a word for the first seasonal offerings to the gods. In a papyrus document, however, it has the meaning of "legacy duty," and in another it signifies the fee demanded for citizenship. In yet another context, it clearly means "birth certificate"; and this would provide a convincing and illuminating rendering for Romans 8:23, though no one, so far, has seemed to use it. The Christian has a birth certificate of the Spirit. The metaphor is not remote from that suggested for Hebrews 11:1. The word used for "collection" in 1 Cor. 16:1 was unknown elsewhere till it appeared in the papyri with Paul's meaning. So too had the verb he used when he told Philemon to put anything owed by Onesimus "on my account" (Philem. 18).

The new light from the papyri suggests, in consequence, numerous more exact translations. For example, read "originator" for KJV's "captain" in Hebrews 2:10, "debating" for "doubting" in I Timothy 2:8, and "I have guarded my trust" for "I have kept the faith" in II Timothy 4:7.

Examples might be multiplied, but enough has been quoted to show that, with the discovery of the papyri, the language of the New Testament has truly risen from the dead.

11

ARCHAEOLOGY AND THE BOOK OF REVELATION

Less than twenty years after Revelation, the last and most difficult book of the New Testament, was given to the church in the province of Asia in A.D. 96, Cornelius Tacitus, Rome's distinguished historian, wrote of the period from A.D. 69 through the death of the Emperor Domitian. He called his book the *Histories*, and wrote it during the reign of Trajan, when such peace as a disguised autocracy could give had come to Tacitus' decimated senatorial aristocracy. The society to which he gave an eloquent voice was still quivering from the tyranny of Domitian's later years, and the fact that Christians shared their suffering could be an indication that plots sparking the emperor's fear-ridden vengeance had, indeed, involved Christians, who had infiltrated the highest ranks (see chapter 9).

Tacitus is of enormous interest in the study of the New Testament, because he wrote with a memory fresh with the evil years when John, surrounded by Domitian's bitter persecution, wrote his letter to the churches of Asia, called the Apocalypse or the Revelation. It was a letter meant to be understood by those who had more clues to its deliberately obscure imagery than have survived the wastage of the years. The allusive, cryptic language belonged to that order of prose-poetry found notably in Daniel, Ezekiel, and Zechariah, which is called "apocalyptic." John's Christian contemporaries would have had the keys to his letter's meaning. The uninitiated would not. In times of persecution by the state, it is sometimes good to use a secret language of symbolism and metaphor to protect oneself from charges of sedition and treason.

Times of persecution they were. The power of the empire was in the hands of the vicious Domitian and was directed against the church. Tacitus knew about the Christians and told of Nero's persecution of them in another historical work, the *Annals*. He did not mention them in the *Histories*; but he did, in his opening chapters, paint a dark picture of the last years of Domitian. In clipped and biting phrases he wrote of the horrors of tyranny, disaster, savage cruelty, vast evil, corruption, murder in high places, and ruinous civil strife. The sea, he said, was full of exiles; and he listed islands where nobles lived out their banished lives. Tacitus might have added Christians and one island more, for John was on "the island that is called Patmos for the word of God and the testimony of Jesus Christ" (Rev. 1:9).

The island of Patmos.

It is possible that John was placed there to save his life. The governor of Asia, as a senator, had no cause to love Domitian; but he had no choice but to obey his decree to persecute the Christians. The letters of Pliny, written to Trajan a generation later, show that the Christians constituted a very considerable minority in Bithynia, the province north of Asia, and no responsible proconsul would be anxious to alienate a sound and disciplined section of his subject population. A considerable number of Christians lived in Asia. Perhaps it was under the proconsul's orders that John went over to Patmos, over thirty miles across the sea; and with permission he kept in discreet contact with his scattered congregations. The Romans called such exile "relegation," and it may well be that John had a good bit of freedom on the oddly shaped island. By banishing John to Patmos but secretly letting him remain in touch with his congregations, the proconsul hoped to appease both Domitian and the Christians. Of course, this is speculation. John may have been in chains and guarded by Roman soldiers.

Unlike the province on the mainland opposite, Patmos has nothing to offer to the student of New Testament archaeology by itself, so redolent of the aged apostle who served the Christians of Asia. That province is uncommonly rich in archaeological remains, some of them invaluable for understanding the book John wrote under Domitian's tyranny. William Ramsay pioneered the study and above all made it clear that the seven letters of the second and third chapters of the Apocalypse were real letters to seven different congregations in an Asia that must have been crowded with Christians.

The Seven Churches

Ephesus

The largest of all sites of New Testament archaeology lies near the Turkish village of Seljuk. Nearby are the stone remnants of Ephesus, the scene of a century of digging. To be sure, archaeologists have uncovered only a small section of the ancient city, enough to make a walkway down to the restored facade of the library, around to the huge theater, across the great axial street, and out. The descending flagged street has the facades of shops and temples cleared, but the mass of the buildings lie still covered at the rear.

Ephesus was one of the early New Testament sites visited by Western travelers in the days of romanticism when travel in the eastern Mediterranean was wild adventure. Rose Macaulay,[1] who has made a fascinating collection of the ruin-literature of travelers and poets, quotes Richard Chandler who visited Asia Minor two and a half centuries ago. "Returning from this cavity," wrote this eager clergyman concerning the swamp, where he thought he had found the temple of Artemis, the Diana of the vivid story of Acts 19, "the traveler has nothing else in view but venerable heaps of rubbish, and must be forced to supply his curiosity with considering that this was the place where once stood and flourished that renowned wonder of the world."

One of H.V. Morton's most colorful chapters[2] tells how at Seljuk he found a stagnant pond, lush with waterweed, from which protruded sculptured capitals and carved column drums. Here he imagined the summer frogs croaking in derision: "Great is Diana, great is Diana," for the mudburied marble is all that is left of the great temple of the mystery cult which kept ten thousand priestess courtesans employed.

John Wood, an architect turned archaeologist, worked at Ephesus for a decade and finally located the theater by following the great street, characteristically axial on the plan of a Greek city. That was in 1870, the year Schliemann found the stronghold of Troy. In the previous year after a six-year search, Wood had found Artemis' temple deep in the boggy silt on the alluvial plain.

The theater had a seating capacity of twenty-five thousand people. The magnificent theater was the scene of the famous riot of Acts 19:21-41 that was instigated by Demetrius the silversmith who made silver shrines of Artemis.

Votive offerings and such tourist souvenirs as the silversmiths made have been found in plenty. Some of these artifacts, which included ivory statuettes of Artemis, were discovered in 1904 by D.G. Hogarth and dated back to troublous times seven centuries before Paul's adventure. Such representations, like figures of Ar-

heater and street leading to the harbor, Ephesus.

temis on Ephesian coins, showed the female figure of the goddess covered with appendages like breasts. It was more probable that the appendages represented bunches of grapes; but, at any rate, they were fertility symbols and relics of the Nature goddess from which the later cult descended. It is quite difficult for us today to imagine the pervasive nature of the idolatry that evoked the irony of Paul in Athens.

Ephesus lay at the mouth of the Cayster between the Koressos Range and the sea. Like all the river valleys around the great blunt end of the Asian continent's westward protrusion, that of the Cayster was the terminal of a trade route which linked with other roads converging and branching out towards the separated civilizations and tribes of the east and the Asian steppes. This was why Ephesus was chosen by the early Ionian colonists from Athens as a site for their colony. The Greeks called a colony an "emporion," or a "way in," because their concept of such settlement was that of a gateway by which an active self-governing community could tap the trade of a foreign hinterland. Ephesus filled the role precisely.

By New Testament times, however, the great days of Ephesus' trade were past. Like her rival Miletus, similarly located at the end of the Maeander valley, thirty miles to the south, Ephesus had difficulty with her harbor, the essential gateway to the sea. Deforestation has been mankind's ancient folly, and no part of the Mediterranean world has suffered worse than Asia Minor. The quest for timber and charcoal, overgrazing, and the destructiveness of the Mediterranean goat, eternally nibbling and trampling the regenerating forest, denuded the hinterland. Topsoil slipped from the bared hillsides, streams became swamps, and the stormwaters reached the sea laden with silt, which choked the harbors. The harbor-works of Ephesus may be traced today seven miles from the sea. Where once a sheltered waterway formed a safe haven, there is now a reedy plain. William Ramsay, most factual of archaeologists, speaks in awe of the "uncanny volume of sound" which, in his day at the turn of the century, greeted the evening visitor to the desolate levels where Ephesus once harbored her ships.

She was, nonetheless, over many centuries, fortunate in her engineers. The winding Maeander was silting up the harbor of Miletus as early as 500 B.C.; and when that city suffered irreparable damage in the Persian suppression of the great revolt of the Ionian Greek cities, the choking up of her waterway passed beyond repair. It was Ephesus' opportunity, and a succession of rulers promoted the maintenance of the harbor facilities which the increased volume of trade and traffic demanded.

The kings of Pergamum, most dynamic and powerful of the lesser successor-states of Alexander's divided empire, did much for Ephesus; and when the Romans inherited the kindom of Pergamum by the will of its last ruler, Attalus III, they continued the policy of promoting Ephesian trade. The Romans took up the legacy of Pergamum in 133 B.C. and used Ephesus as the proconsul's seat. The city was proud of its name, "the landing place;" and the title is found on a coin as late as the third century of the Christian

122

The marble street, Ephesus.

era. It is, perhaps, significant that the same coin bears the image of a small oar-propelled boat, an official's "barge," not the deep-hulled merchant-men which mark the city's pride in her seaborne trade on the coins of earlier centuries. Paul's ship made no call there in A.D. 57.

Domitian, at the end of the first century, appears to have been the last ruler to attempt to repair the harbor of Ephesus; but trade had obviously declined two centuries before. By the time of Justinian, five centuries later, the battle with sand, silt, and mud was lost; and Ephesus was falling to ruins in a swampy terrain. Justinian, to be sure, built a church to Saint John on the site, in part compensation perhaps for the looting of the green stone columns from Artemis' temple for the vast church of Saint Sophia in Byzantium, or Constantinople as the city was then called. They may still be seen by visitors to the great basilica in Istanbul.

Deepening economic depression and decline were therfore the

background of Ephesus' life over the period of the New Testament. If the spirit of a community seeps into a church and determines, in some fashion, its outlook and its testimony, Ephesus provides an illustration; for the stone foundations of jetty and dockside warehouse, deep inland on the edge of the desolate plain, are sharp light on the city whose Christians were bidden be mindful whence they had fallen and do as they once did, where old things had passed away and ahead lay death.

One fragment of archaeological interest in Ephesus not generally mentioned by commentators is to the left of the marble street, which crosses the front of the theater. On the right was a brothel with suggestive signs on the paving pointing the way for clients, and on the left a shoulder-high wall. Panels carved in high relief upon it show Roman soldiers in panoply, in "whole armor" (Eph. 6:11). It is difficult to establish the date for the sculpting and erection of this wall, but if it was there in Paul's day, the origin of the fine passage in the sixth chapter of the letter (Eph. 6:11-17) to the church is revealed. If a reliable dating questions this assumption, the sustained metaphor in the Ephesian letter could conversely indicate that such a decoration in an earlier form may have been visible in the city. This situation is similar to the Apollo temple so prominent in Corinth, which provided a striking piece of imagery in the letters to the isthmus congregation. All the pieces are there, especially in one panel in which the armored legionary stands in battle pose, shield up, sword at the ready, helmet firm, and booted feet firmly placed.

The last glimpse of Ephesus shown in the New Testament reveals an aging church in need of an infusion of new life. Hence the closing detail of imagery in the apocalyptic letter. Coins of Ephesus sometimes show a date palm, sacred to Artemis and the symbol of the goddess' beneficent activity. "I will give [him who overcomes]," writes John, "to eat from the tree of life" (Rev. 2:7). It was not to be. Ignatius, writing a generation later, still accords the church high praise. It became a seat of bishops, and a notable council was held there as late as A.D. 431. Then came long decline. The coast, with continual soil erosion of the hinterland, became malarial. The Turks came with ruin for Asia. The church died with the city. The "lampstand" was removed out of its place.

Archaeology, nonetheless, has shown that the prestige, and indeed the magnificence of the city, long outlived its declining usefulness as a seaport. Under Claudius in the middle of the first century and under Trajan at the beginning of the second, the great theater was remodeled. It was under Claudius that the monumental Marble Street was built. Nero gave Ephesus a stadium. Domitian widened and beautified the great central boulevard. Adornment continued till the days of the Gothic raid in A.D. 263. It is obvious that Paul's vision had picked on one of the strategic centers of the world.

Smyrna

For the archaeologist Smyrna shares the disadvantage that every functioning city shares. The buildings of a living present are in the way of those who seek the remnants of a dead past. Izmir, as Smyrna is now called, is the third largest city in Turkey, with a population of three-quarters of a million or more.

It was a major city in John's day with over a hundred thousand citizens. Information about the city in historical references and in such remains as meager digging has been able to investigate reveals that the origins of Smyrna are lost in prehistory. As in most ancient sites, there were days of decline and revival, the latter especially under the beneficent hand of Alexander.

On the site might be seen parts of the forum of Roman times, bearing out the tradition of Smyrna's importance. Her deep harbor never silted. Perhaps the outflow from the Dardanelles, swift with the current from the Black Sea and the Russian rivers, kept up a semblance of tidal flow and scouring as far as the entrance of the deeply recessed gulf at the head of which Smyrna stood.

Youthful Smyrna was Ephesus' rival, and to Smyrna's enduring church was promised a "crown of life" (Rev. 2:10). The Christian would fasten on the words with satisfaction, for it was the sort of poet's tag on which cities preen themselves. Athens was "violet-crowned," until men tired of the adjective. Of Auckland, New Zealand, where these words are written, to its citizens' delight, Kipling wrote, "last, loneliest, loveliest, exquisite, apart." In such fashion the simile of a crown dominates all praise of Smyrna.

"The city has been styled," writes the Rev. Chandler in his eighteenth-century account, "the crown of Ionia." More significantly Aristides calls the "Golden Street," which ringed Mount Pagus with lovely buildings, "the crown of Ariadne in the heavenly constellation." Apollonius of Tyana, amid rich praise for Smyrna, says rhetorically that it is greater charm "to wear a crown of men than a crown of porticoes."

From afar, the crest of Mount Pagus, its broken ruins cleared by the diligent spades of modern digging, still faintly suggests a diadem above the city's crest. "I have been up there," wrote Freya Stark, "sometimes to walk in the morning, with Ionia on one side and Aeolis on the other, spread below; and nearby, in a shapeless depression, the stadium where Polycarp was burned, and have thought of that old bishop how he would describe his intercourse with John, and with the rest of those who had seen the Lord...." Under "the crown of Smyrna," Polycarp was not the only Christian who won "a crown of life."

Evidence seems to have emerged of a strong Jewish minority in Smyrna. This may account for the strength of the persecution of the Christians the letter foretold, but archaeology has not so far been able to substantiate this. One puzzling reference is an inscription dated about A.D. 123-124, acknowledging a contribution to some public fund from "the one-time Jews." Whether they were Jewish apostates or lapsed Jewish Christians cannot be said. It is not clear whether they could have been "a synagogue of Satan" (Rev. 3:9).

Pergamum

Pergamum, royally situated in a commanding position, with a view of far ranges, the sea, and the purple peaks of Lesbos, had been, when John wrote, a city-seat of government for full four hundred years. It was a capital city in pre-Roman days; and when the last of her kings, Attalus III, bequeathed his kingdom to the Romans in 133 B.C., Pergamum became the chief town of the new province of Asia. It was natural then that the first temple of the imperial cult, the worship of the emperor on which the Christians looked with such deep abhorrence, should be located here. A temple to Rome and Augustus was erected in Pergamum in 29 B.C. So "the worship of the Beast," as the uncompromising imagery of Revelation 20 described it, came to Asia. But other cults beside that of Rome were endemic at Pergamum. There was the worship of Asklepios, the god of healing, whose symbol was a serpent. A coin of Pergamum shows the Emperor Caracalla standing spear in hand before a great serpent coiled around a bending sapling. The emperor raises his right hand in the exact gesture of the Nazi salute, which is, in fact, one of the most ancient of all gestures of adoration. A prayer as old as Psalm 144 calls for rescue "from the hand of foreigners, whose mouth speaks vain words, and whose right hand is a right hand of falsehood." (v.11).

The letter to Pergamum is addressed to those who dwell "where Satan's throne is," and Christians must have found something peculiarly satanic in the town's preoccupation with the serpent image. Pausanias the Greek traveler, who wrote many descriptions of ancient cities, spoke of Asklepios as "sitting on a throne with a staff in his hand, and his other hand upon the head of a serpent." The church in Pergamum must have found the surrounding symbolism of paganism quite diabolical.

Pausanias also mentions the magnificent throne-like altar to Zeus, which stood on the crag dominating the city and which is now in East Berlin. The altar commemorated the defeat of a Gallic invasion of Asia. Recovered by German archaeologists, the great block of decorated stone was taken to Berlin where it forms a major exhibit in the East Berlin Museum, rebuilt after the fashion of twenty centuries ago in a huge silent hall, cunningly lighted. Its base is more than forty yards long and nearly forty wide; it rises to a height of perhaps fifty feet. In form it might be the entrance to some gigantic temple. Above three sides of the base a graceful colonnade runs, set with dozens of slender pillars. A flight of twenty-six wide marble steps rises up to its center, which contains a small sanctuary. Immediately below the colonnade are set the friezes which are the altar's chief glory.

They tell the story of the legendary struggle between the gods and goddesses of Olympus and the giants. Athena, her face long

The reconstructed altar to Zeus, Pergamum.

since obliterated, clutches the hair of a rising giant. Hekate thrusts a torch into the face of another; and there stands Artemis, her shattered arm still poised to hold a bow. The giants, in accordance with Pergamum's prevailing obsession, are represented as a brood of Titans, with snake-like tails. Curiously enough, examination by experts from the British Museum of the battered marble figure of a giant, which has been lying for some years in the junk yard of the Worksop Town Council in a London suburb, has led to a startling conclusion. The statue may be one of the missing figures from the frieze surrounding the altar of Zeus.

This Zeus, to whom the throne-like altar was dedicated, was called Zeus the Saviour; and the title would impress Christian minds as peculiarly blasphemous. They must have called the altar "Satan's throne" and so put the phrase in the Apocalypse. "No wonder," writes Moffat, "Pergamum was called the throne of Satan by early Christians who revolted against the splendid and insidious paganism of the place.... Least of all in this cathedral center of the imperial cult could dissent be tolerated."

But how did the giant from "Satan's throne" get to London's Worksop? Some careful sleuthing appears to establish the fact it came from Asia over two centuries ago to form part of the collection of the Earl of Arundel and fell on evil days when Worksop Manor, the Arundel seat, was broken up.

The statue could have been battered off the great piece of sculpture about A.D. 1000, when the Christians in control of the area defaced this representation of the complete pantheon of Olympus. At this time they seem to have broken up most of the enormous pagan monument, using much of it in their works of fortification.

There are other notable remains: a library, a steep theater, the temple to Trajan, and a gymnasium on the great granite acropolis; but none of these are of Christian significance. One additional point only: why the "white stone" (Rev. 2:17)? The hard, coarse-grained granite is not amenable to the chisel, and so the mass of inscriptions on the height are in imported white marble. The

The ruins of the altar to Zeus, Pergamum.

Christians would understand this, as, indeed, they understood the letter and the whole book.

We could wish that the temple of Asklepios were better preserved. A road as richly paved and columned as that at Ephesus leads to where the temple stood outside the city, a full mile from the foot of the huge hill. There is a plunge bath, for bathing was part of the regime in these great healing centers. There is an impressive covered walkway, but little else remains.

Thyatira

Inscriptions are grist for the archaeologist's mill; and from Thyatira, fourth of the cities of the Revelation, they come in plenty. Thyatira's valley was a broad and ancient highway of trade; and in the days of the Roman Peace the city became, like Laodicea, a center of busy commerce. More trade guilds, those ubiquitous associations of businessmen and craftsmen, have been identified in Thyatira than in any other Asian city. Inscriptions mention workers in wool, linen, leather, and bronze; plus dyers; tanners; potters; and bakers.

The people of Thyatira's church were thus drawn from a commercial community, alive to salesmanship, keen to do business, and alert to capture trade. Lydia, it will be remembered, when she met Paul in distant Macedonia, was a Thyatiran abroad with purple cloth to sell. The trade guilds must have been an anxious problem to the Christian craftsman. How could he attend the formal meetings and banquets without witnessing licentiousness and condoning pagan rites? It was the old Corinthian problem of "eating in an idol's temple" (I Cor. 8:10) which confronted the struggling church. Archaeology, with its revelation of the scope of the city's trade organization, has set the moral dilemma in high relief. But as with Philadelphia and Laodicea, little more than preliminary surveys have been carried out for the excavation of Thyatira. Systematic archaeological investigation may have much more to say on John's seven churches.

The little Turkish town of Akhisar lies over whatever ruins there are of Lydia's hometown. The site gave no clue to the meaning of

"Jezebel" (Rev. 2:20), who seems to have been some advocate of compromise in the difficult world of trade. Nor did it give an indication of the "fine brass" mentioned (Rev. 2:18), which was probably some sort of alloy.

Sardis

Sardis is a beautiful vale beside the Pactolus River, legendary in ancient times for its alluvial gold. The chief impressions of the site for the casual visitor are the laborious restorations of the Jewish synagogue and of the Greco-Roman gymnasium. The spur of Mount Tmolus on which the ancient Lydian and Greek stronghold was built is of interest. So is the uncovered temple of Artemis and the massive Roman Flavian Delphi theater.

Sardis, however, has received some attention from the archaeologists. As early as 1910, the American H.C. Butler, with a magnificently equipped expedition, worked on the site. The great crane

Temple of Artemis, Sardis.

which was used for lifting large blocks of stone lay rusting in the ruins for many years, as its own contribution to the wilderness, after the "dig" was abandoned in 1914. Harvard and Cornell universities have recently continued the good work. Sardis' temple of Artemis has been uncovered. It appears that under the influence of the Cybele-cult of Ephesus that goddess was associated with Artemis in joint worship. It was an unfinished building and has no significance in the interpretation of John's apocalyptic letter, save that a cross cut here and there into the stone shows that the pagan shrine was converted to Christian purposes. The remains of a brick chapel are also visible in the ruin. A mortgage deed, dated some three centuries before Christ, gives some idea of the wealth of the temple. One Mnesimachus acknowledged a huge gold loan and specified whole villages in security.

Philadelphia

The Turkish country town of Alashehir, cosily situated in an offshoot of the Hermus Valley, covers with its dusty and undistinguished streets whatever is left of the earthquake-ridden New Testament town of Philadelphia. As with Thyatira, the present town shuts off the past and leaves archaeology only coins on which to speculate. Coinage, for example, does show that the valiant little community did, in fact, take a "new name" in gratitude to the emperor for disaster relief (see Rev. 3:12). After a great earthquake in A.D. 17, Philadelphia took the epithet of "Neocaesarea" in tribute to Tiberius Caesar for helping rebuild the city. History, geography, and even geology have contributions to make to the elucidation of the cryptic letter, but that does not fall within the scope of this book.

Laodicea and Its Neighbors

Sixty or more miles away across the hills, in the parallel Lycus and Maeander valley, a broad plain between walls of hills, are Colossae, Hierapolis, and Laodicea, near the confluence of the twisting Maeander and the Lycus. They form a ten-by-six-mile triangle and leave the impression that the Christian congregations were as thick all along that strip of river territory as they would be in any similar town and country stretch of farmland in America today.

One can sit at Hierapolis (Pumakkale or "Cotton Castle" today) and look across the river plain rich in history. At one's feet hot silica-laden water flows down a low escarpment to form white, glazed pools of sulphurous water. In the same thermal area there are many springs of chemical-charged water, which prompts the drinker to spit the water from his mouth (Rev. 3:16). This was a symbol of the useless lukewarmness charged against the lethargic Laodicean church.

Hierapolis was a spa and a resort place for the affluent. Heavy Roman remains of public buildings are visible there. Colossae has nothing to show on the subject before us. Its huge mound is unexcavated. Perhaps with time, the Turks will be able to uncover the New Testament cities of Asia as remarkably as they have done the town of Aphrodisias. Some work has been done on the site of the rich city of Laodicea.

Just before Revelation was written a great gate was erected at Laodicea and dedicated to Domitian, whose name was later chiseled off. The foundations are exposed and could give an ironic twist to the words: "I stand at the door and knock (Rev. 3:20). Rich though the stern letter is in historical and geographical reference, its archaeological relevance must await continued and much fuller investigation of the site.[3]

The Beast and Its Number

The most horrific of the visions of Revelation occurs in chapter 13. Two points find some illustration from archaeology, the seal of the beast and the number of his name.

In the papyri, "to be sealed" meant to be imperially protected and retained for imperial use. This appears to be the use of the verb which Paul had in mind in Romans 15:28, a verse which has produced an astonishing variety of renderings. Paul seems to mean: "When I have secured this fruit for them to hold and to retain." Seals were set, in pursuance of this practice, on sacks of grain to guarantee the correct weight or measure of the contents. There was also a mark, a red stamp, which was required for all

The Forum, Rome.

documents of exchange. It showed the emperor's name and the year of his reign and was technically known as "the seal."

If, therefore, the first and basic interpretation of the beast was Caesar himself, John's picture of the seal stamping hand and brow of the duped multitude was shockingly true to life (Rev. 13:16-18). The people were stamped and sealed with the sign of the false god of Rome, stamped upon the hand that creates and before the brain that plans. And without the stamp, which stands symbolically for conformity and tacit acceptance of the worship and divinity of the emperor, a man could not "buy nor sell" (Rev. 13:17). The trade guilds with their stranglehold upon a man's livelihood and the success of his daily avocation, are, of course, in view. This somber century, in which the battle for liberty has been fought over again in three continents and still continues to be fought in large tracts of the globe, has produced many illustrations of the tyranny over hand and head and the despot's threat to livelihood and thought, which John thus symbolized.

And what of the last verse in the chapter 13: "His number is 666"? Note first that a far from negligible manuscript tradition gives 616, not 666. In both Greek and Latin the letters of the alphabet had numerical value, and the fact was very commonly used to build puzzles. Among the wall scratchings from Pompeii is an election notice in which the vowels are cryptically exchanged for numbers, and another inscription speaks of a girl called Harmonia. "The number of her name," is says, "is 45." The key to the puzzle seems to be that Harmonia suggested the nine Muses, and 45 is the sum of all the digits from 1 to 9.

The churches of Asia probably knew the key to 666 or 616, but it was early forgotten. In Greek 616 adds up to "Caesar God," but 666 was not so simple, and much ingenuity and juggling with spelling has been employed to fit the number to "Nero Caesar" or "Caius Caesar." It is also plausibly suggested that 666 falls short of the perfect trinity 777 in all counts, and thus presents a grisly picture of the power and baseness of Antichrist. Archaeology has thus done no more than point the way. The subject remains open for conjecture and ingenuity. After all the writer warns his readers:

"Here is wisdom" (Rev. 13:18). Perhaps some papyrus scrap, still undiscovered or undeciphered, some inscription under a Turkish doorstep or embedded in a wall, contains an answer to John's cryptogram.

The key to the interpretation of Revelation is, of course, the significance of its imagery. Much of that imagery is Old Testament in its origin; much of it, as the illustrations in this chapter have briefly shown, is based on contemporary history and geography. Some of it, it may be fairly admitted, is still elusive; and it is here that archaeology may still have something of interest and importance to say.

Archaeology is no longer a Western preserve. There are indigenous schools of archaeologists in Bible lands, which are doing and will no doubt continue to do good work. Asia Minor, scene of the earliest activities of the organized church, still offers vast scope for investigation and discovery. The Revelation is a document of early church history and as such will yet yield more of its primary meaning, as spade and trowel bring to clearer light the ways of thought and action in the first century.

Ostia on Tiber

The ruins of Pompeii are perhaps not typical of Roman cities of the first century. Pompeii was a country town of no great magnificence. Other towns around the Bay of Naples, which the erupting Vesuvius devastated, were grander than Pompeii, a seaside residential haven of the rich.

Ostia stands apart. Ostia, located at the mouth of the Tiber, was a large trading port where the big commercial ships found harborage. In the "taunt-song" of Chapter 18, John pictures destruction falling on Rome, the Babylon of the Seven Hills, and the lament of the Mediterranean traders who no longer, in that day of judgment, will discharge their cargoes there. It was at Ostia that the ships unloaded; and the great warehouses still stand, their gaunt ruins two and three stories high. So much of what was once Rome itself is covered by the vast building of later ages. Today only enormous monuments stand out. At Ostia, the Tiber port, much still remains to illustrate the wealth of Rome's commerce and the extent of the trade John envisaged in 18:9-19, a passage embedded in the awesome vision of the fall of the beast and the mighty symbols of Rome's power. Those verses are strikingly illustrated at Ostia Antica.

An ancient road, some fourteen miles long, ran down from Rome to her port, already four centuries old in New Testament times, and the object of much imperial attention over that period. The port was the rendezvous and meeting place of the trade of the world.

The extent of the remains abundantly illustrate John's striking words. The houses still stand two stories high and are much more modern in appearance than those of Pompeii. The port must have rivaled Alexandria as a center of Mediterranean trade. Granaries, offices, blocks of apartments, still stand, ruined, yet well preserved in red and yellow brick. They were, as John indicated, a symbol of the commercial power of the empire and the imperial force of the great and organized might of the beast, which rose to crush the young church in the middle decades of the first century.

Travelers usually came to Rome from a similar port on the Bay of Naples, where massive fragments remain. The docks here also could accommodate the big Alexandrian grain ships. Paul went to Rome from Puteoli by way of the Via Cousularis, which joined the Appian Way after about twenty miles at Capua.

Ostia was a much easier and straighter path of access for heavy cargoes to Rome than Puteoli, so John's denunciation in chapter 18 can hardly have been any port other than Ostia.

The first Christian remains go back to about A.D. 200, but Ostia became a notable Christian center. Here Monica, Augustine's mother, died just as the two were awaiting a ship back to Africa. In his *Confessions* Augustine told the story of his last talks with Monica.

> She and I stood alone leaning in a window which looked inward to the garden within the house where we were staying, at Ostia on the Tiber.... There we talked together, she and I, alone, in deep joy.... we were discussing in the presence of Truth, which is You, what the eternal life of the saints could be like.... But with the mouth

of our heart we panted for the great waters of your fountain, the fountain of the life which is with you: that being sprinkled from that fountain according to our capacity, we might in some sense meditate upon so great a matter.

Within a week Monica was dead.

Ostia was, in fact, near the end, which John so vividly pictured. After the cataclysmic attacks of the Vandal hordes, which Augustine escaped by his death in A.D. 430, and as the barbarian warbands closed in on his episcopal see at Hippo, Ostia died along with Rome itself.

NOTES

[1] *The Pleasure of Ruins*, p. 235.
[2] *In the Steps of Saint Paul*, pp. 320-340.
[3] The cities of Revelation are dealt with at greater length in *The Cities of the New Testament* by E.M. Blaiklock (Pickering and Inglis).

12

THE SURPRISE OF THE DEAD SEA
SCROLLS

The days of archaeological discoveries that catch the wonder of the world are not yet past. The last few years have added the discoveries of the rich tombs of the Macedonian kings and the city of Ebla to old tales of romance, such as Layard at Nineveh, Carter in the Valley of the Kings, and Schliemann at Troy. Recently added to this list of discoveries is the saga of the Dead Sea Scrolls.

Few places in Israel are visited by more tourists than the fortress of Masada at the southern end of the Dead Sea and the equally somber ruins of Qumran at the northern end. Not far from Qumran is Jericho, with its palms and jacarandas on the floor of the Jordan Rift Valley. Here the hopeful tourist can follow Naaman and expose dermatological lesions to the chemical-laden waters and the lengthened ultraviolet rays. A few miles further down the road, which winds a trifle claustrophobically under the tumbled mass of the rugged Judaean wilderness, lies Qumran. A hot, uncanny place, Qumran is far below the level of the Mediterranean Sea and was once the wilderness home and refuge of a sect of Jewish ascetics.

The Scrolls

In 1947, just before the bloodshed and turmoil which led to the foundation of Israel, the hidden documents of the desert sect were discovered accidentally in some of the caves that pock the cliffs be-

Qumran, Cave 4.

hind the ruins of the ancient settlement. This was a find relevant to both Testaments. A wandering Bedouin shepherd boy, a flung stone, and the faint clatter of broken pottery were the first events in a story of an archaeological find, which may be justly counted as the most amazing biblical discovery of the century. It is also a story of scholarly tenacity, sheer courage, meticulous research, and devotion on the part of Western and Israeli scholars.

Perhaps no other discovery quite equals that of the Dead Sea Scrolls for its breadth of relevance. Its superb Isaiah Scroll, which could have been handled by John the Baptist, is safely housed forever in the Shrine of the Book in Jerusalem. Its more recent gospel fragments perhaps reveal written evangelical memoirs of the sort to which Luke refers in his preface (vv. 1-2), which many have sought to put in order.

In comparison to the Dead Sea Scrolls, few documents have been more intensively studied and, indeed, more recklessly interpreted. Some hostile critics with interest in eliminating the influence of Christianity and the challenge of Jesus Christ have ludicrously asserted that the teaching of the Qumran sect disposes of both. The organ of the Russian Communist Youth, Komsomolskaya Pravda, at one time alleged that the scrolls proved that Jesus never existed! The English Hebraist, John Allegro, wrote syndicated newspaper articles that claimed the Dead Sea documents as "a challenge to the Church far greater than was ever presented by Darwin's theory of evolution." The naive and foolish theory advanced in Allegro's subsequent book about an alleged "cult of the sacred mushroom" abundantly deserved the crushing blow delivered by a dozen academic authorities, Christian and non-Christian, in a letter to the *Times* in May 1970.

Of course, stripped of hysteria from both sides, Darwin's theory was never "a challenge to the Church," and neither were the Dead Sea Scrolls. The notion that Christians were somehow afraid of

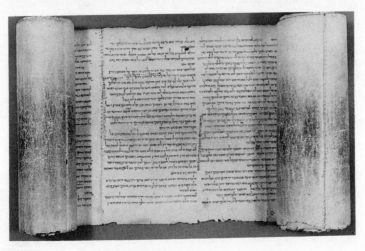

The Isaiah Scroll, columns 32-33.

disconcerting revelations destructive to their own beliefs and documents never had validity. F.F. Bruce, who has written more sense about the discovery than most authorities, ironically recalled how he read a paper in 1955 to the Society for New Testament Studies only to read in a popular treatment of the scrolls by Edmund Wilson a few weeks later that "New Testament scholars have almost without exception boycotted the whole subject of the scrolls."[1] The charge still persists.

The Teacher of Righteousness

The texts from the caves are varied. There are manuscripts of Old Testament books, a thousand years older than anything scholarship had hitherto possessed. There are commentaries on the prophets of no great value. There is a "manual of discipline," from which it is possible to gain some notion of the life lived in the desert community. There is a strange mystic story of a war between "the children of light" and the forces of darkness, with some allusion to a "Teacher of Righteousness" done to death by the hierarchy.

This mysterious figure at first gave rise to some controversy. As far as substance can be given to the shadowy personality, the Teacher was probably the founder of the sect, a good man who rose in protest against the corruption of religion and met the martyrdom such saints too commonly encountered in man's somber story. To identify him with Christ, who died in the full blaze of recorded history, only demonstrated the eagerness of some to diminish at all costs the historicity of the founder of the Christian faith. Nor did the people of Qumran think of their Teacher of Righteousness as a messiah. In their odd eschatology they regarded themselves, in some sense, as the corporate fulfillment of Isaiah's "Servant" and Daniel's "Son of Man." They looked for the appearance, at the end of the age, of three figures: a priestly messiah, a military messiah, and Moses' "prophet." But critics hostile to Christianity, in the first extravagances of interpretation, thought they had discovered the real origins of Christianity. How anyone could imagine the blurred and elusive Teacher could be the reality and the tremendous figure of Christ, whose record has daunted mankind, could be a legend based on him passes understanding.

Some ingenuity has been more legitimately expended in attempts to identify the Teacher and his chief persecutor, the "Wicked Priest," with known historical figures. No conclusive identification has been reached; but it is ludicrous to see the crime of the collaborating priesthood, so starkly described in the Gospels, as being in any way a rendering of the fate of the Teacher of Righteousness. More than one noble person was put to death by vested interests, religious and political.

The Qumran Community and Christ

Some of the Qumran sectarian expressions might be found in the utterances of Christ, but surely a teacher of the common people of the land would be expected to seek a vocabulary close to that of contemporary religious usage. The imagery of light and darkness, so common in John's writings, and phrases like "eternal life," the double "amen," or "verily, verily I say" do appear in the Scrolls, but this only demonstrates that Christ spoke the common language of his day. Christ's way was to emphasize old truth and set it in a more compelling light. In precisely the same way Paul adapted and appropriated the terminology of the "mystery religions."

In direct contrast with the rigid discipline of the Qumran sectaries, Christ was no ascetic. His foes held that against him. He also contradicted their ethical teaching, notably in His firm command to love one's enemies. Qumran counseled hate for "the foe of light." "Love the Children of Light," advised the Qumran text, "and hate the Children of Darkness." This is an order from the allegorical document found among the Scrolls; "The War of the Children of Light and the Children of Darkness," a curious compilation built out of the detailed study of the Old Testament wars, plus what appears to have been a Roman military manual. Nothing could be more alien to Christ's teaching. Indeed, he was surely admonishing such a sentiment when he said: "You have heard that it was said: 'You shall love your neighbor and hate your enemy,' but I say to you, love your enemies" (Matt. 5:43,44).

In short, it is historically impossible to identify the well-documented life of Christ with the exotic allegorizing of the desert sect. Kevin Smyth, the Jesuit scholar, remarked that to compare the scrolls with the New Testament is "like comparing a fish and a man because both are wet after coming out of the sea." And against those who saw in Qumran the soil from which Christianity sprang, Smyth said: "Rather it was from the soil such as this that sprang the thorns which tried to choke the seed of the Gospel." Smyth was perhaps overemphatic, for, traced up and through John the Baptist, dissident Essenism of which Qumran was a facet, might in fact be granted a place in pre-Christian history. Its measure of good was taken, absorbed, and interpreted in Christian attitudes and thought. But the majestic center of the new faith was solely Jesus Christ.

The Gospels—Superior Documents of the Ancient World

Those who are emotionally committed to an anti-Christian view are in difficulties with the Gospels. To say, as Allegro did, that "there is no worthwhile contemporary evidence outside the New Testament that Jesus ever existed," is no contribution to discussion. The four words "outside the New Testament" strip the assertion of meaning. Historians would be glad to have evidence so authentic, so multiple, so congruent, on more than one personality and event of ancient history.

The evidence of the Anglo-Saxon irruption into Britain is confined to a few score words in the Venerable Bede. The evidence of Julius Caesar's reconnaissance across the English Channel in 55 B.C., a date which every schoolboy used to know, is principally in Caesar's own words in a document designed to justify his military career. The simple existence of the English people, like the existence of the church, has a certain verificatory force.

The Gospels, however scholars might disagree on this detail or that, are obviously documents of ancient history. A papyrus fragment from the last of them to be written can still be seen in a Manchester University library. This document was palaeographically dated in the first generation of the second century. The first account of the life of Christ is reliably dated in the middle sixties of the first century. A mere myth could not grow in a historically documented age. The classical historian is perpetually amazed at the methods of interpretation tolerated in New Testament scholarship, which would be dismissed as absurd in any other branch of historical study. The letter already referred to in the *Times* of London in 1965 on the subject of the Scrolls was signed by six Old Testament scholars of professional rank and shows that such amazement is not confined to classicists.

When the little band at Qumran fled before the Roman cohorts who were mopping up the pockets of resistance in the lower Jordan valley, Christianity was already established in Alexandria, Antioch, and Rome. Perhaps in A.D. 68 the patrols found and burnt Qumran. That was the last year of Nero's reign. Four years earlier, Nero had made the Christians of Rome, "a vast number" according to Tacitus, the scapegoats for Rome's great fire. Almost twenty years earlier, if the Nazareth Decree is rightly judged a rescript of Claudius, Nero's imperial predecessor had heard the Pharisees' explanation of the empty tomb. Seven years earlier still, the same Claudius had chided the Jews of Alexandria for turbulence and apparently made reference to Christian missionaries. But these are trifles. The career of Paul of Tarsus, heir of three cultures and ranked for intellect by the great classical scholar T.R. Glover with Plato, had ended before Qumran went its pathetic way.

As scholars went to work in Qumran and its library they found that the true interest and meaning of their discovery lay in the ruin, as much as in the caves, and in the people, as much as in the Scrolls. But the study of the community of Qumran really added little to what was plain for all to see in the New Testament. The Scrolls merely sharpened vision and understanding. Another discovery might serve as illustration: All visitors to Stonehenge today can see a typical short-bladed Mycenaean dagger carved on one of the upright stones. This carving was located by photography in 1952 but had been there 3500 years. No one saw it until it was pointed out. Now it is obvious to all.

The situation is similar to the Scrolls. Most of what they reveal was plain in the Gospels, but few had seen the historical truth until the study of the Qumran society enlivened understanding.

The "Third Force" in Palestine

The Pharisees and Sadducees are prominent in the gospel story. The first-named were the defenders and exponents of the law; the second were a cynical priestly hierarchy, collaborators, and simonists. Both hated Christ—the Pharisees because He exposed the hypocrisy of their legalistic pretensions,—the Sadducees because He menaced their profits and their comfort. But there was a "third force" in Palestine, a pure core of faithful folk who kept true religion alive in an age of disillusionment and worldly materialism. These people were the New Testament representatives of what the Old Testament calls "the remnant," the seven thousand who had not bowed the knee to Baal (I Kings 19:18), "God's poor," the faithful in all ages.

Mary and Joseph, and the parents of John the Baptist, belonged to this group; so did the Bethany family; so did the fisher-folk of Galilee, the erstwhile disciples of John; so did the widow in the treasury who dropped a tiny contribution into the box. They were all there in the story, quite clear to the reader. The Scrolls seemed to give them life. Among them the old tradition of the wilderness was alive, and this is another feature of the New Testament on which the Scrolls form a commentary. The wilderness requires a word of fuller explanation.

The Role of the Wilderness

Deep in the Hebrew consciousness was a distrust of the city. Abraham, with the vision of monotheism in his heart, had left Ur of the Chaldees, the great pagan seaport on the Persian Gulf, because his purpose was to found a nation in the clean and empty wilderness. His was a sound instinct, and the Hebrew consciousness saw the action for the symbolic movement it was. The writer of the Epistle to the Hebrews wrote in a familiar style when he pictured Abraham, the father of their race, "dwelling in tents with

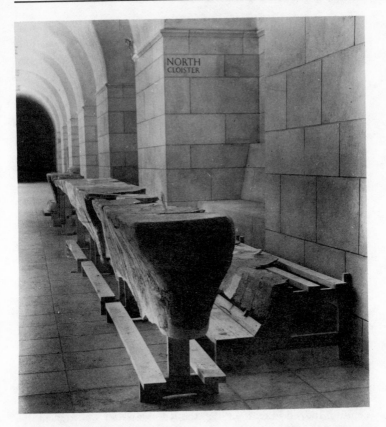

Writing tables from Qumran.

Isaac and Jacob, the heirs with him of the same promise; for he waited for the city which has foundations, whose builder and maker is God (Heb. 11:9,10).

So, too, in times of national stress, the wilderness suggested itself to the Hebrew mind and made their rallying cry: "To your tents, O Israel." And during the Feast of Tents, every year the city dwellers forswore their comfort and lived on rooftop and in garden in tents or shelters of palm branches. All through history, too, urban religion, smug and formal and prone to corruption, was never safe from the brusque intrusion of an Amos, or an Elijah, men of the wilds and the empty countryside. Such men were swift and ruthless in denunciation of sin and urgent in calling an errant city multitude back to the simplicities of faith.

Not surprisingly around the time of Christ a protest movement again sought the wilderness. Isaiah's writings are prominent among the Scrolls, and a verse from Isaiah could have been the marching order and directive of the Qumran community. "Make straight in the desert a highway for our God" (Is. 40:3).

Nor can it be an accident that these very words find echo in the recorded sayings of John the Baptist. He was a voice that cried in the wilderness: "Prepare the way of the Lord, Make His paths straight" (Mark 1:3). The fervent desert preacher, whose whirlwind ministry forms a prelude to the Christian story, was obviously under the influence of the desert religious communities or perhaps a member of one of them. His activities were centered a dozen miles from Qumran. His disciples, who became Christ's "fishers of men," were converts who went back to their daily ways of living and carried into industrial and urban life the breath of their wilderness devotion.

The Historians and Qumran

The fact that there was a protest movement in Jewish religion has always been known. The Essenes were described in the first century. Indeed Pliny the Elder, the Roman writer whose scientific curiosity led him to his death in the eruption of Mount Vesuvius in August, A.D. 79, actually described a community by the Dead Sea, which could easily be the people of the Scrolls. He had doubtless talked with many soldiers who had fought through the Jewish War of A.D. 66 to 70, during which the community of Qumran was broken up, leaving its library in the sheltering caves.

Pliny's account of the Dead Sea contains the following paragraph. This passage led to a major archaeological discovery.

On its west side [Pliny referred to the Dead Sea], just far enough from its shore to avoid its baneful influences, live the Essenes. They form a solitary community, and they inspire our admiration more than any other community in the whole world. They live without women, for they have renounced all sex life; they live without money, and without any company save that of the palm-trees. From day to day their numbers are maintained by the stream of people who seek them out and join them from far and wide. These people are driven to adopt the Essenes' way of life through weariness of ordinary life and by reason of the change of fortune. Thus, through thousands of generations—incredible to relate—this community in which no-one is ever born continues without dying; other people's weariness of life is the secret of their abiding fertility. Below their headquarters was the town of Engedi, whose fertility and palm-groves formerly made it second only to Jerusalem; but now, like Jerusalem itself, it lies a heap of ashes. Next comes Masada, a fortress on a rock, itself also not far from the Dead Sea. And there is the frontier of Judaea.

Typical of a too common kind of Victorian skepticism, Hastings' *Dictionary of the Bible*, in an article of over eighty years ago, dismissed Pliny's account of an ascetic community by the Dead Sea as mistaken. With the library from the caves to point the way, the archaeologists turned to a ruin at Qumran and found it to be just such a place as Pliny described, a sort of monastery but without celibacy, as skeletal remains of both men and women revealed. Qumran was the home of a dedicated fellowship given to discipline, the preservation of the Scriptures, and to holy living. The community was established about 135 B.C. It continued for almost exactly two hundred years. In A.D. 66 came the mad revolt of the Jews against the Romans, over three years of grim and awful warfare, the destruction of Jerusalem, and the systematic ransacking of Palestine for all remnants of Jewish opposition. To the Romans, in the days of the great revolt, such folk were partisans; and Vespasian's troops overran and destroyed the buildings. The inhabitants, no doubt, escaped, for they had time to hide their books in the caves. "But we have this treasure in earthen vessels," said Paul (II Cor. 4:7), and he was alluding to a custom observed at Qumran. The books were concealed in great jars of earthenware.

Qumran and Christian Origins

Here then is a vivid, if not quite accurate Roman picture of a Jewish community remote from the urban preoccupations and practices of the hierarchy of the Sadducees and the twin schools of Pharisaism. This community was one of many such groups, with associates throughout the land, by no means all of them remote and separated from the tasks of industry and daily living. Implicit in the Gospels, too, was the fact that Christ sought His first followers and disciples among the poor of the land, outside organized religion.

Here lies the meaning of the Dead Sea Scrolls for Christians of today, which may be summed up in three exhortations. Let them seek simplicity in their faith and avoid the perils of social compromise. Let them find unity in a common devotion to their God. Let them be prepared to see the blessing of Heaven rest rather on the devoted than the proud, on the humble rather than the great.

But such was never the theme and purport of the New Testament. If Qumran is, in Edmund Wilson's phrase, to rank with Bethlehem and Nazareth as "a cradle of Christianity," then in this sense the tendentious words could be true. John the Baptist translated passive protest and retreat into action, withdrawal, and return, if historian Arnold Toynbee's formula might be applied. And because John's converts provided the first Christian disciples and prepared the land for the impact of Christ, Qumran, if John was influenced by the group, might claim a preparatory part.

The Scrolls and Biblical Studies

Textually the Scrolls provided some enlightenment concerning Old Testament studies. They cleared up a handful of inconsiderable textual corruptions and threw light on some minor difficulties of interpretation. Until 1947, for example, the oldest text of Isaiah was dated A.D. 895. A major item among the Scrolls is an Isaiah manuscript a full thousand years older. What was its impact?

There is, for example, no break between chapters 39 and 40. How, in the light of this, was the theory to stand, first propounded in 1892 by Bernhard Duhm, that there were three Isaiahs (the first Isaiah ending with chapter 39), conflated and fused in the first century? Here is a book, dated at the latest about the end of the second century before Christ, which obviously knows nothing about it.

Some individual texts were also cleared up. Consider Isaiah 21:8, which, in the King James Version, is quite without meaning. "And he cried, A lion: My Lord, I stand continually upon the watchtower in the daytime...." Realizing that Hebrew was originally written in consonants only, the vowels were inserted later, imagine the effects of the system. In English so written "bt" could be, according to the context, but, bet, abet, beat, about, boat, and so on. "Lion" in Hebrew is built as RH, which properly vowelled reads *ariah*. But "he who saw" is *raah*, which without vowels was similarly RH. Some early scholar vowel-pointed the word wrongly and produced "a lion." Read then: "And he who saw cried: My Lord...." Sense was surely restored to a tormented text.

There is another mistranslation due to incorrect vocalization in Isaiah 49:12. The older versions spoke of the land of "Sinim," which could only refer to China. To the disappointment of those who cherish so far-flung a text, the Scrolls showed that the reading should be *Syene*, which was Yeb in Upper Egypt. In 20:1, the proper name Tartan, which occasioned some difficulty, read in the Scroll *turtan* and was correctly rendered in RSV as "commander in chief." Add a brief phrase in 53:11, where the Scroll followed the Septuagint rather than the Masoretic text on which our Bibles were based, and you have all the differences. The conclusion is that the Isaiah Scroll, by and large, demonstrates the astonishing accuracy of the text, which has been transmitted to us.

The Isaiah Scroll also demonstrates the accuracy of the Septuagint, clearing up in the process a New Testament text. In Acts 7:14, Stephen remarked that Jacob's tribe came to Egypt, "seventy-five people." Genesis 46:27, on the other hand, said "seventy." This was a contradiction beloved of critics like the nineteenth-century orator Robert Ingersoll. A Qumran text of Genesis read Stephen's figure. Hebrew numerals are delicate to write, and Stephen's correct quotation became corrupted in the later manuscripts behind our version.

Again, what did Christ mean when he blessed the poor in spirit? A Qumran text shows that the phrase was used in religious parlance as the opposite of "the hard-hearted." Pity, it might be said, came into the world with Christ. Perhaps the people of the Scrolls had seen a glimmering of that light.

The Qumran story, however, is not yet ended. The archaeologists are at work, and much more may be heard of the true patriots of Palestine and the stratum of society from which Christ called his first disciples.

Apart from such pieces of notable usefulness, the Scrolls offer little else of significance. There are commentaries. One, for example, on Habakkuk, but the exposition was symbolic and mystical and remote from modern thinking and the plain meaning of the text. There are some biblical romances, embroiderings of the Old Testament story, of no more value than the lighter literature of the religious bookshop of today. They have no interest to the New Testament scholar save that they show what might have been the lighter reading in the schools of Judaism in which the first Christians received their education.

NOTE

[1] F.F. Bruce, *Second Thoughts on the Dead Sea Scrolls* , p. 138.

13

ARCHAEOLOGY AND THE TALE OF THE JEWS

The western coast of the Dead Sea is a stretch of rugged shoreline full of history. Qumran, at the northern end, has already engaged our attention. Halfway down the coast, the oasis of Engedi, David's old refuge in the days of his wilderness exile, has its opening to the sea. The Essenes had a center there, unless Pliny, in the passage mentioned in the last chapter, was actually referring to the Qumran community. But continue farther south and to the west across a barren plain studded with mean thorn bushes where the salt-caked ground crackles beneath the feet. Here appears a crag, flat-topped like Capetown's Table Mountain and notched at its sharp northern end. This is the fortress of Masada, whose story has been told often enough in recent years, notably in a vivid television mini-series. Masada's story illustrates the fate of those who chose Barabbas, the path of violence, and consequently the ghastly clash with Rome that devastated the Jewish nation.

The most awful wars of the first century were the Great Rebellion of A.D. 66 to 70 and its equally bitter sequel in A.D. 132 to 135. Archaeology can add some striking chapters to the shocking story, and this account of the archaeology of the New Testament might fittingly continue with episodes of the Colosseum, Masada, and the Bar-Kochba relics.

The Colosseum

Italy's largest ruin, the Colosseum, is in danger, according to recent surveys, of falling into yet greater decay. The vandals of Renaissance days, who used the building as a quarry, weakened its structure sadly; and much money will be required to restore it. The old pile looks sturdy enough. Penetrate the tunneled arcades, which provide entrance, and one is amazed at the vast size of the blocks of stone of which the lower walls are built. To look down on the dark oval from an incoming airplane on a steely winter afternoon is to gain a deep impression of its cruel strength. The aircraft sweeps down toward Rome and the Ciampino airfield. There is first the Tiber snaking through the pastel-shaded countryside, yellow with the silt of Tuscany; then, sharply, Rome, more compact than most other major cities with its great apartment houses, which were a feature of Rome in ancient times. Then the observer notices the semicircle of Saint Peter's majestic forecourt, the tasteless Victor Emmanuel monument, and the tumbled forum. And nearby is the great jagged molar of the Colosseum, a surviving symbol of that harsh, forgotten world.

Called the Colosseum in the Middle Ages, the Romans named it the Flavian Amphitheater, after the Flavian imperial family who raised it on the site of the lake in the gardens of the Golden House, which was the huge, mad palace Nero was building when he came to his grisly end in A.D. 68. The next year, A.D. 69, saw chaos, with four imperial rivals striving for power on the trampled soil of Italy. Vespasian, the candidate of the Syrian legions, engaged at the time in the bitter struggle of the Jewish rebellion, emerged as conqueror. Vespasian came to Rome, leaving his brilliant soldier-son Titus to finish the war in Palestine with the long horror of the siege and destruction of Jerusalem, which was one of the grimmest pages of all ancient history.

In Rome, paying attention to the urban mob an emperor could not afford to neglect, Vespasian began to build the Colosseum and formally opened two levels in A.D. 79. Vespasian died in that same year. In the two brief years of his reign, Vespasian's son Titus added a third level and the upper arcade, the familiar circle pierced with windows, which still survives in part. The finished amphitheater must have been an amazing building. Its timbered floor covered a labyrinth of rooms, dens for wild beasts, mechani-

The Colosseum (Flavian Amphitheater), Rome.

cal elevators, and an elaborate drainage system. An intricate network of exits, entrances, numbered corridors, and stairways enabled a marshaled multitude to pass in and out with speed, smoothness, and precision. Forty thousand spectators were accommodated.

The Arch of Titus, Rome.

Detail from the Arch of Titus showing the candlelabra being taken from the Temple in Jerusalem.

But consider the dates. Jerusalem fell in A.D. 70, and in blood and fire the wild revolt was quenched. Jewish prisoners flooded into Rome. They might be observed still, carved on the triumphal arch of Titus, marching behind the conqueror's chariot with the looted seven-branched candlestick from the temple of Jerusalem plain to see above their heads. Thousands of despairing Jews must have toiled on the Colosseum, cementing its cruel pile with their blood.

Masada

But when Titus marched home in A.D. 70 to his hard-won triumphal celebrations in the capital city of the Roman Empire, he left a blazing pocket of resistance behind him. Jerusalem itself was a pile of calcined stone. The seven-branched golden candlestick was stored with Rome's loot in the Temple of Peace, there to stay until the Goths carried it off in A.D. 410, burying it with dead Alaric in the bed of the Busento, diverted for the purpose. But down by the Dead Sea a band of Zealots and Daggermen were under desperate siege on Masada.

Who were they, these spiritual descendants of Barabbas, the terrorists of the Jericho road, the Sicarii, or "men of the dagger," and the Zealots, one of whose society, a man named Simon, became a disciple of Christ? Some of the determined garrison might have been Essenes or members of the Qumran community thirty miles farther up the Dead Sea coast. This may be the meaning of a "Qumran-type" scroll the excavator Professor Yigael Yadin described which came to light during the 1966 excavation of Masada. The Roman patrols of Vespasian overran and obliterated Qumran in A.D. 68. If some of their community retired to join the remnant on Masada, there might perhaps be substance in the Roman belief that the Qumran complex was a potential stronghold of guerrilla resistance. That the ascetic community would have given shelter to fugitive resistance fighters was inevitable. Peaceful though it might itself have been, the community could have been taken over by more desperate fighters. And some of the Qumran writings were not without a coloring of armed revolt.

Masada.

Professor Yadin spent three years of scientific archaeological investigation and reconstruction on Masada. He uncovered Herod's
two palaces on the level summit of the great crag, the Roman
camps, and the whole plan of the mighty siege and assault. The
results appeared, superbly illustrated, in Yadin's great book *Masada*, published in 1966. This research confirms the story told at laborious length by the historian Josephus. This sly and clever man
had been guerrilla commander in Galilee at the outbreak of the revolt, but had been defeated and captured. By a shrewd playing of
his cards he had won, not only freedom, but a post as secretary in

the immediate entourage of Vespasian. Josephus then used his leisure to write the story of his people.

Herod's Fortress

The stronghold of Masada was one of three mighty forts built in the rugged eastern hills of Judaea by the first Herod, who ruled the Jews as a puppet king of Rome from 40 to 4 B.C.. The other two forts were Herodion and Machaerus. Masada was fortified in 36 B.C., over a century before Rome ended the great siege. In this almost impregnable place, it is possible to glimpse Herod's fear-haunted soul and the shadow of the deepening paranoia that

The Herodian.

darkened Bethlehem (Matt. 2:16). The fort was mightily built of casemate-wall and battlement. Reservoirs, huge enough to hold fourteen million cubic feet of water, cleverly channeled out for the flash floods, that are a feature of the violent climate, were chipped out of the solid core of the rock. One of the royal palaces stood on the projecting southern promontory of the summit plateau, skillfully built on three different levels, with a sheer drop beneath. Hence the phrase "the hanging palace," which recurs in Professor Yadin's account. This construction was a magnificent piece of architecture and engineering, a Roman palace, complete with bathhouse and hypocaust, the very symbol of Herod's pro-Roman policy. Allied with subtle concilation of the Jews, the able Herod family pursued such a policy successfully for a whole century. Wine jars, stamped with the name of C. Sentius Saturninus, consul for 19 B.C., told the same tale of skillful collaboration. The jars were marked: "To King Herod of Judaea," the first inscription ever discovered containing Herod's name. The wine was evidently Augustus' present to the useful Jewish king. The view across the sinister waters of the Dead Sea was superb and appropriate. A secret staircase, "the serpent path" mentioned by Josephus, had helped in the identification of the vast ruins.

This path, wrote the historian:

> ...is broken off at prominent precipices of the rock, and returns frequently into itself, and lengthening again by little and little has much ado to proceed forward; and he that would walk along it must first go on one leg and then the other; for on each side is a vast, deep chasm and precipice, sufficient to quell the courage of everybody by the terror it infuses into the mind.

Jesephus decribed, with details of area and length, the fortifications and architecture of Herod's fortress and its two royal abodes, making him so dry to read, but a blessing to archaeologists. He described, too, the storehouses of dates and corn laid up for a siege, all of which, he alleged, remained edible and fresh for long years in the rock reservoirs. Remnants have been found in the long storerooms. The stronghold was well-stocked and well-armed when it fell into the possession of the last desperate Jewish fighters of the

Great Rebellion. Ablaze with nationalistic fervor, the nation only fell back beaten when the ashes of Jerusalem covered a million dead and the land had been combed systematically at appalling cost of toil and blood. Titus went home for his triumph, while a remnant retired to the fortress, which rebels had seized at the first outbreak of war, and prepared to fight it out. Titus left his general Silva the task of taking the stronghold, without saying too much in Rome about the last valiant band who were holding out in the Judaean wilderness.

Mass Suicide

The memorials of the Roman siege are still clearly visible on the site. The wild Jewish garrison was ringed in by such walls of circumvallation as those Julius Caesar so often described in his war commentaries, and the lines of the digging and heaping of the earth remain discernible around the base of the escarpment. The two Roman camps may also be seen. Against the cold methodical tactics of Roman engineers and storm troops, the world's valor always proved vain. Masada followed Carthage, Capua, Alesia, and other cities, which had learned by grim experience the firm and unrelenting pressure of a Roman siege. Inevitably, the end came. The Roman ramp, heaped and piled with dogged toil against the great cliff, climbed higher and higher. The covered siege engines rolled up its steep slope. The stone ballista balls, catapulted from their armored tops, poured into the fortifications. They were found later in piles. At last the battering rams began hammering the final wall. The garrison built another wall of beams behind it, but it was fired in their faces. The end had come.

Josephus' story of the storming makes grim reading. Eleazar, the captain of the Jews, gave two long speeches in which he exhorted his followers to cheat the victors by mass suicide. There is something peculiarly horrible in his assembling of moral and theological argument, and the Jewish historian reported it all at merciless length. The men embraced their wives and children and cut their throats. They set fire to their last possessions in the corners of their rooms. Ten men were chosen by lot to slay the rest. These lay down by the bodies of their families, and the ten executioners went systematically to work. One man was then chosen by lot out of the ten, and he killed his nine companions. The very lots, fragments of pottery bearing the names of the ten, found, the letters still legible on the baked clay. The lots were thrown, no doubt, into a helmet, and one was drawn. Left alone in the charnel house, the lone survivor went around the ranks of the dead and made sure with a thrust here and a slash there that none remained with a vestige of life; and then, reported Josephus, the last man drove his sword through his own body.

On the steps of Herod's smaller bathhouse there were the remains of three bodies. The excavators moved the rubble with care. Masses of plaques from scale-armor spoke of a soldier's corpse. Nearby was the skeleton of a young woman, her scalp intact in the dry atmosphere. Her dark hair beautifully plaited, looking as if it had been newly braided for the day of death. The plaster of the wall nearby was stained with blood. Delicate lady's sandals were on the steps, and nearby was the skeleton of a child. Was this the last man alive, dying finally by his own sword, after killing wife and child?

So fell nearly a thousand Jews. But two women hid five children in remote cellars and concealed themselves with food and drink. When the Romans staged their final assault, burst in, and paused in wonder and suspicion at the awful solitude, these survivors came out and told what had happened. The Romans themselves, wrote Josephus, "could take no pleasure in the deed."

Palestine then lay in such peace as only a war of annihilation could give. A Roman garrison apparently occupied Masada after it had held out incredibly for almost three years after Jerusalem had fallen. "They make a desert and they call it peace," said a bitter British chieftain in Tacitus' account of Agricola's raid into northern Britain in A.D. 79; and after the fall of Masada, Palestine was desert indeed. How any further resistance could be possible is difficult to imagine; and in fact, no resistance to Rome's ruthless rule arose in Palestine for over two generations.

The Bar-Kochba Rebellion

What Hadrian did not realize, sixty years after Titus, was that the ruin-pile of Jerusalem was a matter of sentimental, indeed of fierce religious interest, to the remaining Jews of Palestine. Throughout the world they had again been restive, prey to waves of passionate nationalism. In Trajan's reign, seventeen years before, the great Jewish populations of Cyrene, Alexandria, and Cyprus had risen against their Greek neighbors and killed them in hundreds, only to suffer reprisals as fierce and bloody.

In Hadrian's day revolt was localized in Palestine. Hadrian had conceived the idea of rebuilding Jerusalem. The city's ruin offended his tidy mind and artistic spirit. On the temple site he proposed to build a shrine dedicated to Olympian Zeus. Nothing could be more calculated to inflame the Jews, and it is odd that the most traveled of the emperors had been so ill-informed about the depth and power of surviving Jewish sentiment in the devastated land.

With frightening unanimity, Palestine rose. One Bar-Kochba emerged, a "Messiah of the wilderness," the perennial peril of the passionate land. So unexpected was the explosion, so fanatical its leadership, that Bar-Kochba was for a time actually master of the land; and Jewish coins were marked variously: "Simon Prince of Israel;" "For the Freedom of Jerusalem;" and "For the Freedom of Israel."

Again it took the methodical Romans three years of bitter, agonizing guerrilla war to flush the bands of wild Jewish rebels from the tangled hills, ravines, and caves, which had once sheltered David. Losses were appalling. Half a million Jews fell, and Judaea was again left a wilderness. So heavy were the Roman's own casualties that Hadrian, in his report to the Senate announcing the end of the war, omitted the usual introductory formula that stated all was "well with him and with his army."

A cache of Bar-Kochba's letters and campaign documents have been discovered in a cave by the Dead Sea. The documents are in varied scripts, so we might not have the guerrilla leader's own handwriting. Adjutants were, no doubt, the scribes. "Whatever

Emperor Hadrian (A.D. 117-138).

Elisha says, do," ran one command. Another ordered the arrest of Tahnun Ben Ishmael and the confiscation of his wheat. Another called for punishment on some who had repaired their homes, in defiance of some scorched earth policy. Bar-Kochba's orders were all very cold, hard, and infinitely pitiable.

Ten of the letters have been deciphered. They were signed "Simon Bar-Koziba," the hero's name before he took the messianic title "Bar-Kochba" meaning "Son of a Star." Knowing his race, Christ himself had given warning against such dangerous claims:

> Then if anyone says to you, "Look, here is the Christ!" or, "There!" do not believe it. For false christs and false prophets will arise and show great signs and wonders, so as to deceive, if possible the elect....if they shall say to you, "Look, He is in the desert!" do not go out (Matt. 24:23-26).

The words were lost on the brave, doomed Jews of Hadrian's day. Christ's followers, long since noting the warnings, had left the storm centers of Jewish nationalism and found manifold homes abroad. Therefore, few Christians perished in the two rebellions, which reddened two separate decades with carnage.

There was another fragile discovery, which throws pathetic light on this tragic rebellion. A small bundle of papyrus documents, of the sort previously described, was found tied with a palm-fiber rope in a Dead Sea cave. The bundle was packed in a goatskin bag along with some beads, a mirror, and a comb—a whole toilet set, in fact, including perfume and powder container. These articles were the property, perhaps, of the wife of a patrol leader in the stern wilderness war.

14

ARCHAEOLOGY AND THE EARLY
CHURCH

We followed the story of the Jews who fought to their grim and desolate ending in the fierce and heroic resistance movements that left their memorials, such as Masada, by the Dead Sea. But what of the Christian church? We looked at what archaeology has to say of its first beginnings in our analysis of the Nazareth Decree and the church communities of Greece and Asia Minor, but to illustrate the amazing story of the Christian faith our study must move beyond the first century. In Acts, Luke left an unfinished story with Paul at Rome. What of his confrontation with Nero? What of the host, of whom Tacitus wrote, who suffered under Nero's sadism in A.D. 64? Whence came the multitude of Christians who crowded Bithynia early in the second century?

Archaeology has much to say about them, and the final chapter of this book will deal with the amazing story. It is to be forever deplored that we have not the third book Luke must have intended to write when he left Paul at the beginning of a crowded story. There are hints of Paul's activities in the letters he wrote from Rome, but imagine what a historian like Luke would have written about the defense in the high court of the Empire. The case may have lapsed for want of documents, but we have Paul's own word for his lonely "first hearing" (II Tim. 4:16). But this is part of the reason why archaeology is so important for the history of the church outside and beyond the record of the New Testament.

The Appian Way (Via Appia).

Rome was an older city than Athens; and an intimate glimpse of the sad and crowded metropolis with its mingling of glitter and glory and poverty-stricken slum, from a Christian writer, would have been fascinatingly interesting.

Luke's account of Paul's journey to Rome concluded:

> ...We circled round and reached Rhegium. And after one day the south wind blew; and the next day we came to Puteoli, where we found brethren, and were invited to stay with them seven days. And so we went toward Rome. And from there, when the brethren heard about us, they came to meet us as far as Appii Forum...(Acts 28:13-15).

Over the last miles of the long pilgrimage the apostle trod the ancient cobblestones of the Appian Way and moved through a pageant of Roman history. If Paul's spirit was "provoked within him" as he viewed the monuments of Athens and saw the city "was given over to idols" (Acts 17:16), he must have felt a similar emotion amid the clustering monuments of Rome.

The Prevalent Cynicism of the First Century

The "queen of roads," the Appian Way, ran south from Rome; and along its length stand the crumbling tombs of the proud families who fed on the fat of Rome's dominion. Such greed was a barren joy. The worn Latin on the stone is full of the weariness of the age. *Misce, bibe, da mihi,* runs one ("A cocktail, please for you and me"). Another reads, *Somno aeternali* ("In eternal sleep"), and shows with the words the symbol of the inverted torch. "What I ate and drank I have with me; what I have left I have lost," commented another. "Wine and lust ruin the constitution, but they make life, farewell."

Such cynicism marks the age, and Matthew Arnold's verse fits a multitude of illustrations.

On that hard pagan world disgust
And secret loathing fell...

World-weariness was rife. Catullus, poet of high society in the days of Julius Caesar, wrote:

Suns may rise and set again, but for us eternal night remains for sleeping.

"Fruitless words on dust which cannot answer,"[1] he sobbed over his brother's grave. This was the stern friend of Cicero, writing in those days when the Republic was crumbling. The great orator's daughter was dead, and Sulpicius sent consolation.[2]

Here, he says, is a little thing which may comfort you. On my way back from Asia I travelled by sea between Aegina and Megara, and I began to look at the regions round about. Behind was Aegina, Megara was in front. On the right was Piraeus, and on the left Corinth, towns once in the glory of their strength, which now lie broken before our eyes. This is how my thoughts began to run, "Ah! We little men are hurt if one of ours should die! Yet the wonder is we live so long when in one place the corpses of so many cities lie." Provinces, my friend Cicero, are being shaken. Why, in such a day, be so moved if you have become the poorer by the frail spirit of one poor girl?

No wonder Byron called Sulpicius "the Roman friend of Rome's least mortal mind."

The cultured Hadrian, who built the mighty wall across Britain, put the same pessimism into his little poem:

Odd little comrade, comfortable guest
Capricious elfin puff of air,
You're off; But where? And when you've left my breast
Tense little traveller, pale and bare,
Will you find anything to laugh at there?
(trans. Geoffrey Household)

The Optimism of the Early Church

But move on a few generations, and some indication of the transformation wrought by Christianity is found in a similar context. Under Rome, deep below the Appian Way, run the ancient catacombs. They were cut through the soft tufa rock, a network of galleries encompassing the city and even acting as a cushion against earthquake shocks. In them are multitudes of Christian graves, and countless inscriptions record the faith of men and women.

Here lies Ulpia in a small recess. She needed little room, Ulpia, who "sleeps in peace," as the inscription puts it, for she is but a handful of bones, whose fragments perhaps tell how she died. Her friends wrote on the stone that she had not been buried, but "decorated." Hard by, a marble slab records the fact that Eutychia, "happiest of women," lies beneath. A locket with her body depicts Christ bearing the fruit of the tree of life, and above is cut the outline of a strong, sweet face. In strangest paradox the corridors of death contained all that was truly living of ancient Rome. In the simple art and wall inscriptions is the warmth of hope and faith. Pagan Rome above the catacombs was in the Indian summer of her imperial strength. Storm was brewing in the vast hinterlands of the twin continents, and all the Caesars had built and fought for was to pass in ruin. All that had been worthwhile in Rome's great story was to be preserved for another age by those who bore their martyred dead to burial in the dark tangle of the catacombs.

The Catacombs—An Art Gallery of Belief

The life of the early church, the cherished beliefs of its men and women, their favorite stories, their heroism and endurance is recorded vividly in the graffiti and simple art of the catacombs. Those persecuted generations, vibrantly alive, and unaffected in their devotion, seem in every way more intimately near to us than generations of Medieval Christians who filled Rome above with churches and somber art.

William Henry Withrow, a nineteenth-century writer, remarked[5] on the complete avoidance of all images of suffering and woe, or of tragic awfulness, such as abound in sacred art above ground.

> There are no symbols of sorrow...nothing to cause vindictive feelings even toward the persecutors of the Church; only sweet pastoral scenes, fruits, flowers, palm branches, laurel crowns, lambs, and doves; nothing but what suggests a feeling of joyous innocence as of the world's golden age.

Wider areas of these amazing galleries should be open to the Christian public. Serious archaeologists nevertheless did fine work, and some of their findings are a striking contribution to the history of the church. This is notably true on the vexed question of the strength of the first Christian communities in Rome, for on this subject the catacombs have a clear and authoritative word to say.

The Lateral Growth of Early Christianity

Consider first the "lateral" spread of the church. The adjective is James Orr's, whose striking Morgan Lectures delivered at Auburn in the State of New York, first made many Protestants aware of the historical significance of the Roman catacombs. Orr's lectures, in fact, published in 1899 in a modest volume titled *Neglected*

Factors in the Study of the Early Progress of Christianity, merit, like many others of his apologetic writings, a generous modern edition.

Reliable calculations suggest that the vast tangle of the catacombs contains several hundred kilometers of galleries. The lowest estimate of the graves is 1,750,000; an admissible probability is something like 4,000,000. This is obviously a question that could be settled quite conclusively. At any rate some ten generations of Christians are buried in the catacombs. Thus, on the second figure, a Christian population, in and about Rome, of 400,000 for one generation is probable. On the smaller figure this would be 175,000.

Such averaging, of course, is not good statistical method, for the number of Christians was smaller in the earlier, and larger in the later, generations of the period concerned. But if the figure of

Artwork within the Catacombs.

175,000 is taken as representing a middle point in that period, say about the middle of the third century after Christ, those who remember Edward Gibbon's estimate of the Christian population of Rome will immediately mark a huge discrepancy.

Gibbon's guess, recorded in his *Decline and Fall of the Roman Empire*, was that the Christians at the end of the third century numbered something like one-twentieth of the population of Rome, estimated at something like one million. The most conservative interpretation of the catacomb burial figures would, therefore, suggest that not one-twentieth but one-fifth of Rome's people in the middle Empire were Christians; and possibly, the proportion was at times much greater.

And what of the Roman world at large? The quite impartial archaeological evidence is confined to the capital; but it was a close-knit world, with the gospel moving through the main centers of population, from the East progressively to the West. Gibbon believed that the Christian minority was fairly evenly distributed, and that seems likely. If, therefore, what was true of Rome was also true of Carthage, Alexandria, and similar main cities, other evidence should be considered. The fiery Tertullian, who spoke for North Africa at the end of the second century, should not, for example, be lightly dismissed.

In spite of state action, large numbers of the Christians were exciting pagan alarm in Rome. "The killing beast that cannot kill," of Edwin Muir's moving poem, had done its worst without avail. "Men cry out," wrote Tertullian, "that the State is beseiged; the Christians are in the fields, in the forts, in the islands; they mourn, as for a loss, that every sex, age, condition, and even rank, is going over to this sect;" and, "the temple revenues are every day falling off; how few now throw in a contribution." And speaking in brave defiance before the Proconsul Scapula, where exaggeration could only be bad argument, he maintained:[4] "Though our numbers are so great—constituting all but a majority in every city, we conduct ourselves in quietness and modesty." Tertullian also wrote that if the Christians in Carthage were to present themselves in a body before the governor's tribunal, the governor would have to decimate the city to make an example of them.

The Catacombs.

In the context of such claims, made before authorities in a position to deflate mere rhetoric, must be placed the same speaker's celebrated outburst:

We are but of yesterday, and yet we have filled every place belonging to you—the cities, islands, castles, towns, assemblies, your very

camps, your tribes, companies, palace, senate, forum—we leave you
your temples only.

Throughout many generations of the three pagan centuries, the
Christian community formed a larger proportion of the whole than
the regular church-goers of Britain or America do today. Admittedly the social cleft between Christian and non-Christian was
deeper and more pronounced, but the church could in no sense be
looked upon as an unimportant minority. Christians might have
felt the pressure of pagan contempt, but they never needed to feel
alone. From at least A.D. 200 onwards, they had reason to regard
the future as theirs and to rejoice in the growing strength of the
church.

The Vertical Spread of Christianity

The catacombs also provide illustration of the vertical spread of
the faith in society. Viewing the church at Corinth in the middle of
the first century and speaking with some irony of its tendency toward a false intellectualism, Paul was constrained to say that their
numbers contained "not many wise according to the flesh, not
many mighty, not many noble" (I Cor. 1:26). This remark, which
referred to one church only, was quite illegitimately extended to
the whole. The Gospels and the New Testament generally show
that Christianity, from the very earliest times, invaded the ranks of
the middle and upper classes and touched the intellectuals. As
James Orr wrote:

"It may be going too far to say, with Professor Ramsay, that Christianity 'spread at first among the educated'; but this is nearer the
truth than the opinion often expressed that Christianity drew the
great bulk of its adherents in the earliest times from persons of the lowest and most servile positions—that, in Gibbon's well-known
words, the new sect was 'almost entirely composed of the dregs of
populace—of peasants and mechanics, of boys and women, of beg-
gars and slaves.' "[5]

Consider, for example, the case of Pomponia Graecina, wife of
Aulus Plautius, who won military fame in Britain. Tacitus re-

ported[6] that this noble lady was tried before a domestic tribunal on a charge of entertaining a "foreign superstition." That the lady concerned was a Christian was long ago suggested, but failing other evidence the suggestion remained in the realm of conjecture.

That evidence was supplied by De Rossi, most indefatigable of the explorers of the catacombs. From epigraphical testimony he established the fact that the crypt of Lucina was connected with the aristocratic Pomponian family, one member of which bore the very name of the person mentioned by Tacitus, in its masculine form— Pomponius Graecinus. De Rossi suggested that Lucina (which may be rendered "Lady of Light") was a Christian name assumed by Pomponia Graecina at baptism and that she was the owner or founder of the vault bearing the name.

And if Pomponia was, in fact, a Christian, because she lived on into the reign of Domitian, she might have played a major part in two aristocratic conversions of which there is some evidence— those of Flavius Clemens, the consul, and Domitilla, his wife. The former was the cousin, and the latter the niece of Domitian himself.

Another pagan historian provided the clue. Dion Cassius informs[7] us that Flavius and his wife were accused of "atheism," a common allegation against Christians, and of "going astray after the customs of the Jews." Flavius Clemens was put to death and his wife banished. Eusebius adds his word of testimony, asserting that Flavia Domitilla was exiled for confessing Christ. By an obvious error he called her the niece of the consul. He meant, or should have said, of the emperor.

De Rossi appears to have established the Christianity of this illustrious pair. He discovered the crypt of Domitilla; and whether the lady was the person of Cassius' notice or Domitilla's niece, the existence of a catacomb crypt under the name is sufficient to confirm the Christian connection. Add the discovery of an elegantly constructed "crypt of the Flavians," and Adolf Harnack's contention that "an entire branch of the Flavian family embraced Christianity," is established. These facts furnish startling illustration of the extent to which, by the close of the first century, Christianity had pushed its conquests. Next to the emperor himself, Flavius

Clemens and Domitilla held the highest rank in the Empire; their two sons had even been designated by Domitian as his heirs to the purple. Concerning such conversions James Orr wrote, "ere the last Apostle had quitted the scene of his labours, Christianity were about to mount the seat of empire!"

Society in general was permeated by the Christian faith at a very early period of the church's history. The church admittedly was neither better nor worse for the social standing of its members. Indeed, in the New Testament documents themselves, Corinth was castigated for its pretentions to philosophy and Laodicea rebuked for the harmful influence of its wealth. The world of the early church was such a world as the church knows today, where people of all ranks felt the attraction of Christianity and mingled in the exercise of their faith. We have already mentioned a letter from a Roman governor to the emperor in which he described the grip of Christianity on the province in his charge. He wrote of "all ages, all ranks and both sexes" who had embraced the new faith. The world of the early church was a spiritually hungry world, craving for the consolations of religion. The faith from Palestine ran through Roman society like a prairie fire.

The ancient world in many ways was not very different from the world of today, anxious, war-ridden, disillusioned. Can Christianity do again what it did before? As Professor Butterfield, the great Cambridge historian, remarked,[8] we are in many ways back in the religious situation of the first century, which provides us often with indications of how we should act.

Mithraism—a Rival of Early Christianity

There was a strong rival to the Christian faith in the first centuries of its expansion, and archaeology has added fascinating information for consideration.

In the autumn of 1954, from the bombed ruins east of Saint Paul's Cathedral in London, emerged a little shrine of Mithras, the Persian god of the sun. The existence of this shrine had, indeed, been long suspected. Many years before a piece of Mithraic sculpture had been found not far away in Bond Court by the

Wallbrook. The fragment came from a statuette of the god and bore the inscription: "Ulpius Silvanus, discharged soldier of the Second Legion, pays his vow."

Ulpius was no doubt up from Monmouth, where the Second Legion was quartered, and visited the shrine of the soldier's god as a modern visitor to London might attend divine service in the Abbey of Saint Paul's. In some nearby shop in the crowded streets of the Roman town, he would buy his votive offering and present it to the deity for life preserved. For Mithras was peculiarly the god of the legionaries, brought from the Middle East by the Syrian legions. The swelling notes of the hymn to Mithras, sung by thousands of lusty voices as the sun came up, probably chilled the hearts of a Roman army waiting to defend northern Italy.[9] The legions from the east had marched down through the northeastern passes and were beneath their standards in the camp opposite. This was in A.D. 69, when the Roman occupation of Britain was recent news. When Ulpius Silvanus paid his vow, the religion had first found acceptance with the garrisons of the Middle East and was widely disseminated through the whole Roman army. Archaeology, and quite notably in Britain, demonstrated the fact.

The London Mithras shrine is one of a series. There is another on the Welsh border; another lies somewhere under the walls and buildings of York, still awaiting discovery. On Hadrian's Wall, the ruins of which still run from Newcastle to Carlisle, there are two that are known to us. One is in a cave at Borcovicium. This Roman camp sits on the crags twenty miles from Hexham, near the little village of Wall-on-Tyne. The wall runs in long, firm sweeps over the cliff-tops in this area. This is the best preserved portion of Hadrian's great engineering work; and here, on a southward-sloping hillside, Borcovicium still shows its streets, walls, the foundations of its granaries, and the worn cobblestone, which speak eloquently of the Roman's four centuries of sojourn in the British Isles.

On the slope below the camp is the cave housing the Mithras chapel of the garrison. There is little left to indicate that the legionaries once worshipped here; but one inscription has come to light, revealing the depth to which the cult touched the soldiers' emo-

Mithras, found at Newcastle-on-Tyne.

tions. "To the best and greatest god Mithras, the Unconquerable, Lord of the Ages, Publius Proculinus, a centurion, dedicates this, for himself and his son, in discharge of a vow willingly and rightly made."

The second of the two shrines on the Roman wall is of greater interest. Indeed, its discovery is quite as striking as that of the London shrine. The shrine is at Carrawburgh and came to light accidentally.

The season of 1949 was quite remarkably dry; and with the shrinking of a peat bog the outlines of a little place of worship came to light, which was immediately recognized as a Mithraeum. Realizing that winter would again flood the ruins, the late Professor Ian Richmond, the discoverer, made hasty arrangements for a competent team to examine it. The work was a triumph of modern archaeological research, for the shrine was, after all, not built of brick or stone. It was a modest structure of lath and plaster, and fragile remains of the sort are uncommonly difficult to interpret and explain. The archaeologists nevertheless succeeded. They were able to demonstrate the periodic destruction and restoration of the temple, as Mithraism or Christianity won the ascendancy among the commanding officers of the local garrison. Archaeologists were able to show that the building was finally destroyed in the time of Constantine, when the empire became officially Christian. The archaeologists' uncanny sleuthing was able to show that the floor of the aisle was strewn with heather, that pine cones were used to make an aromatic altar-fuel, and that chickens and geese were eaten in the ritual feasts associated with the cult.

Kipling's picture was true. He imagined a Roman soldier standing sentinel on some high watchtower of the wall. North lay the gray, dreary moors (as they lie below Borcovicium still), with their steely tarns forbidding in the heather. All manner of evil seemed to lurk in the northern wastes, which Rome never surely conquered; and the soldier's heart was full of those ancient fears common to all men who grasp their weapons and peer out into the night. The sun sprang up, and the legionary lifted his spear in salutation as the trumpets rang out from guard post to guard post:

Mithras, God of the Morning, out trumpets waken
the Wall.
Rome is above the nations, but thou art over
all.
Now as the names are answered, and the guards
are marched away,
Mithras, also a soldier, give us strength for
the day.

In the early Persian religion, where his figure first appears, Mithras, like the Roman Jupiter, was associated with light. He was one of the powers of good, who struggled against the forces of darkness and evil. To associate him with the sun was natural, especially at its rising. Mithras, the legend said, had sprung miraculously from a rock and first found worship among the shepherds of the countryside. After his birth, said the myth, the god set out on a series of toilsome adventures like the Greek Heracles. Chief among these was his contest with a mysterious bull, which he captured and sacrificed. Mithraic sculptures always stress this incident and seem to imply, by the expression on the god's face, that the sacrifice was a hard and painful duty.

A Mithras shrine was discovered at Dieburg in Germany. This shrine is decorated with a series of wall sculptures depicting scenes in Mithras' life. A pair of horses of obscure significance comes first. A second curious picture appears to show the Evil One lying in wait for the hero. The third panel is more clear. It shows the birth of the god from the rock. The doings of the god in panels four and five are again beyond interpretation. The incident of the sacred bull fills six, seven, and eight. Panel ten shows Mithras making his alliance with the sun, while eleven and twelve show Mithras ascending the sun's chariot and going to Heaven. A temple of Mithras in Rome developed this last theme more fully.

Christianity's Ascendancy Over Mithraism

If Publius Proculinus from Borcovicium, or Ulpius Silvanus from Caerleon, could walk into a modern Christian church on Christmas Day they would find a few details oddly familiar. They would find some significance in the Communion service. They would find the adoration of the shepherds in hymn and carol something within their experience. The day, December 25th, would be undoubtedly their own. This day, Mithras' birthday, was captured by the Christian church. Christ was not born in December, for shepherds did not watch their flocks by night, "all seated on the ground," in midwinter Palestine. In the fourth century, with Christ's real birthday long since forgotten, the church placed the Nativity Feast on December 25th to overlay both Mithras and the gay Saturnalia.

First it built up a corpus of written records. These documents contained, as Angus, the authority on the mystery religions, pointed out convincingly,[10] something none of the rival cults could match. This was the compelling reality of a historic Christ, much more appealing than the legendary Mithras with his strange conflicts. The Christian documents contained, too, a simple and relevant body of doctrine, adapted for preaching, evangelism, and the needs of daily life.

Secondly, Christianity was universal. Mithraism was for men only. Christianity brought a charter of freedom for women, children, slaves, and outcasts. The Christian faith had food for the hungriest hearts.

Thirdly, a point quite strikingly illustrated by the discoveries at Carrawburgh, Christianity staked all on salvation by faith. In Mithraism, the devotee progressed painfully from rank to rank in the seven degrees of initiation by stern ordeals. At Carrawburgh a coffin-shaped stone cell beneath the altar is large enough for the body of a man. There those who sought acceptance or advancement with the god Mithras endured the ordeal of heat. The fire blazed on the altar, and underneath the human worshiper endured the demons of claustrophobia and scorching pain.

Anything more fundamentally different from the religion of Christ would be difficult to imagine. Mithraism appealed to the soldiers' desire for a leader; it touched their courage and spirit of endurance, but Mithraism was more like a secret society than a faith. It left untouched the vast problem of Evil and failed to satisfy the deepest yearnings of man. Repentance, faith, and brotherly love to all men were outside its teaching. Perhaps is why the great uplifted cross of Saint Paul's now commands the spot where Mithras' shrine lies in ruins.

NOTES

[1] Catullus, 5:4, 5; 101:10.

[2] Cicero, *Fam.* 4:5.

[3] *The Catacombs of Rome*, p. 227.

[4] Tertullian, *Ad Scap*, 2. See James Orr, *op. cit.* Ch. II.

[5] *Op. Cit.*, p.96.

[6] *Ann.* 13:32.

[7] 67:44. See Orr, *op. cit.* pp. 117 sqq.

[8] H. Butterfield, *Christianity and History*, p. 135.

[9] Tacitus, *Hist. III.* 24.

[10] S. Angus, *The Mystery Religions and Christianity.*

INDEX

184

INDEX

ISBN 2-215-08393-X
© GROUPE FLEURUS, 2005.
Dépôt légal à la date de parution.
Conforme à la loi n ° 49-956 du 16 juillet 1949
sur les publications destinées à la jeunesse.
Imprimé en Italie. (04/05)

Zoé et la générosité

Conception :
Jacques Beaumont
Texte :
Fabienne Blanchut
Images :
Camille Dubois

EDITIONS
FLEURUS

GROUPE FLEURUS. 15-27, rue Moussorgski, 75018 PARIS
www.editionsfleurus.com

Zoé n'aime pas donner !
Ce défaut n'est pas très beau !

Mais quand elle devient une petite Princesse
Parfaite, Zoé est généreuse ! Faire des
cadeaux, prêter, ça la rend très heureuse !

À l'école, Zoé garde tout pour elle :
ses biscuits et ses mirabelles !

Mais parfois Zoé est une Princesse Parfaite !
Elle partage volontiers son goûter.

Zoé fait des échanges.
Et encore…
quand ça l'arrange !

Mais parfois Zoé est une Princesse Parfaite ! Elle donne à Mattéo tous ses Lego. « Comme tu n'en as pas, tu peux les emporter chez toi ! »

Les invités ne dormiront
pas ici ! Zoé ne veut pas
prêter son lit.

Mais parfois Zoé
est une Princesse
Parfaite ! Elle veut
bien qu'Axelle
dorme chez elle.
Enfouies sous
le duvet, elles
se racontent
de petits secrets.

Zoé veut toujours
commander. Les jeux,
c'est elle qui les choisit !
Et si Babette fait
la tête, tant pis.

Mais parfois Zoé est
une Princesse Parfaite !
Elle laisse ses copines choisir.
Dînette ou marelle ?
Ce qui compte, c'est
de faire plaisir !

Pour Zoé, ses poupées,
c'est sacré !
On peut regarder
sans toucher…

Mais parfois Zoé est
une Princesse Parfaite !
Elle prête ses jouets sans râler.
Pas la peine de s'énerver.

À la cantine, il n'y a qu'avec les épinards
que Zoé n'est pas avare.
« Qui veut ma part ? »

Mais parfois Zoé est une Princesse Parfaite !
À Fabien, qui a toujours faim, elle donne
une bouchée de son dessert préféré !

Même ses vêtements
qui sont trop serrés,
Zoé a du mal
à s'en séparer.

Mais parfois Zoé est
une Princesse Parfaite !
Elle veut bien donner ses
habits trop petits à sa cousine Lucie.

Zoé joue seule sur le sable mouillé.
Pas question de céder son seau, même
pour construire un château.

Mais parfois Zoé est
une Princesse Parfaite !
Elle prête sa pelle, son râteau
et son tamis. Sur la plage, c'est
si facile de se faire des amis !

Mais quand son petit frère Adam est né,
Zoé a bien changé. Elle lui a tout donné :
ses peluches, son doudou, ses jouets.
Pour Adam, Zoé est toujours une Princesse
Parfaite. C'est génial de devenir l'aînée !